Mastering LinkedIn

For Professional Lead Generation

Monte Clark & Andreas Ramos

Monte Clark
Andreas Ramos

Copyright Notice

Mastering LinkedIn for Professional Lead Generation by Monte Clark and Andreas Ramos. All rights reserved. © 2019 by Monte Clark and Andreas Ramos USA. This document is protected by copyright. No part of this document may be reproduced in any form by any means in any language or any universe not yet discovered without prior written permission from the authors.

About this Book

- *Mastering LinkedIn* was published August 5th, 2019 worldwide as print paperback and ebook
- ISBN 9781086166200
- The audiobook is coming. Send us an email and we'll let you know.
- If you find errors or have suggestions, let us know
- The book's URL is andreas.com/book-linkedin.html

About the Authors

- Monte Clark has worked in marketing for over twenty years. He has worked with Fortune 100 companies and started four companies. He was the VP of Marketing at QTS. He also speaks frequently at conferences and events. He consults with B2B bizdev lead gen teams to use and manage LinkedIn Sales Navigator. Monte was also the technical editor of *#TwitterBook* by Andreas Ramos. Visit him at MonteClark.com
- Andreas Ramos has written fourteen books about SEO. He is an adjunct professor of digital marketing at California Science and Technology University (CSTU) and teaches at INSEEC, the DMA-NC, and AcademyX. He was the Manager of Global SEO at Cisco and director of the digital agency at Acxiom. He lives in Palo Alto with his wife and cat. Visit him at andreas.com

Connect to Us on LinkedIn

- Monte Clark at LinkedIn.com/in/MonteClark
- Andreas Ramos at LinkedIn.com/in/AndreasRamos

Acknowledgements

- Many thanks for valuable suggestions from (alphabetically) Fabrice Palumbo-Lui, Howard Dernehl, Karen Hu (especially for the image on page 5!), and Marianne McGlynn
- Cover design by Monte Clark
- Layout by Anaximander Katzenjammer
- Soundtrack by Brandi Carlile, First Aid Kit, Coeur de Pirate, Zaz, and Eliza Rickman

Trademarks

Names of organizations, companies, and products are trademarks, registered trademarks, or trade names of their respective holders, and have been used in an editorial fashion only. Infringement, endorsement, or affiliation isn't intended.

Promotional Consideration

We mention organizations, companies, software, books, and so on because they're useful for you. We aren't compensated by them in any form.

Dedication

For my wife, who has stood beside me through an amazing and many times trying journey. Who, no matter the season, is faithful. I love you!
— Monte

Table of Contents

USE LINKEDIN FOR INBOUND AND OUTBOUND MARKETING	5
USE YOUR LINKEDIN PROFILE FOR INBOUND MARKETING	10
USE YOUR COMPANY PAGES FOR INBOUND MARKETING	32
USE YOUR CONNECTIONS FOR INBOUND MARKETING	37
USE POSTS AND ARTICLES FOR INBOUND MARKETING	45
USE LINKEDIN SALES NAVIGATOR FOR OUTBOUND MARKETING	66
USE LINKEDIN ADS FOR OUTBOUND MARKETING	97
EXTRAS FOR LINKEDIN: CRYSTAL	117
SUMMARY: SO… WHAT'S NEXT?	126
IN CLOSING	130

Use LinkedIn for Inbound and Outbound Marketing

There are many ways to look at LinkedIn. We use the model of inbound/outbound marketing.

In general, there are two strategies for making business connections:

- Inbound marketing: You attract leads. They come to you. For this to work, you must be visible and findable so your leads can find you when they search.
- Outbound marketing: You find leads. You reach out to them. To do this, you must have a clear idea of who you want to reach so you can work effectively.

Whether people come to you or you reach out them, you build relationships that lead to business and further connections. LinkedIn helps you with this.

Inbound Strategy

An inbound strategy for lead generation (lead gen) works when:

- People want information and they see you have that information
- People want connections and they see you have those connections
- People have a problem and they see you may have the solution

Inbound marketing is essentially self-centered, but in this case, it's the others who are self-centered. They don't come to help you. They come because they see you can help them.

This is the reverse of many approaches to marketing: In outbound marketing companies act self-centered because they just want sales. These companies are acting like a mousetrap and customers are considered the mice.

Inbound marketing flips the relation around to put the focus on the customers, who in this case are your potential connections. You attract them because you have what they want. They're behaving like the mouse and you're offering the cheese. In this way the customers are being offered something they want, something of value.

With inbound marketing you entice customers by offering excellent and exclusive cheese. Your cheese is the best on the market and it's available only from you. Do this by building your personal brand, your expertise, authority, trust, and a strong network of connections in your field. You offer quality content and you actively engage in your field by talking with people, speaking at events, writing articles and books, and so on.

This also includes visibility and creates a reputation of expertise and trustworthiness. That means you stand out to your potential audience. You should show up at the top of searches.

Outbound Strategy for Business Connections

An outbound marketing program is the opposite of inbound marketing. In this case, you're the mouse and someone else is the cheese. You want what they have.

- They have information and you want that information
- They have connections and you want those connections
- They have solutions and you want those solution

There's a bit of contradiction here. Many will say, but that's hypocritical: you're offering something but only because you really want something. In the end, you're the winner.

Indeed, many people are self-centered and approach the market only because they want something. A friend of ours is a career consultant for CEOs. She was working with a CEO who had lost his job and she said, "You need to build a network." The unemployed CEO yelled, "But I don't need a network! I need a job!"

Ah, there was the problem. Why didn't he have a job? Because he had no friends to help him.

The leading people in every field have learned this: the more you give, the more you get in the way of connections, information, projects, jobs, and so on.

Some would say that it's not a strategy: it's just being helpful to others. You offer information, leads, connections, and help people. That works.

- Know who you want to reach. There are only twenty-four hours in a day, seven days in a week, and 645 million people in LinkedIn so you can't reach everyone. In your field, you want to reach the right people who will buy your products or services. Pick the industry, job title, decision-making capability, location, and so on for those whom you want to connect and interact

- Define what they want to see, find and value. What information, connections, or solutions do they want to have? Say it clearly and quickly, in four or five words in plain language.

- Show that you have what they want. Wave your cheese at the mouse.

If you see that you're being ignored, it's likely a problem with your offer. Improve your offer to get better results.

How you present your offer also matters:

- Write in an appropriate style for your audience that will stimulate interest and engagement

- Make sure your website, LinkedIn profile, and other social profiles (Twitter, Facebook, and so on) present an appropriate face to your contact. At nearly every job level now, people will search for you in Google and see what comes up. Your website should be professional and informative. No broken links, no bad grammar, spelling, or punctuation. Your social media pages should be appropriate to your audience. Many organizations use software that lets them quickly review and grade a person's social presence, including inappropriate images, words, and sentiment analysis.

It's not a question of choosing inbound versus outbound: successful people do both.

How to Use Inbound Marketing in LinkedIn

To get others to come to you, you will develop a strong presence in LinkedIn. This means a full profile, company page, postings, and articles. You also get lots of engagement (such as likes and comments) for your posts and articles. People will then notice and come to you.

How to Use Outbound Marketing in LinkedIn

To find others, you use LinkedIn Sales Navigator. This is LinkedIn's advanced search with filter tools to find contacts, learn about the person, put them in groups, follow their activity, contact them, and track your contacts.

We'll cover outbound marketing on LinkedIn in the chapter on Sales Navigator. You'll learn how to find contacts, learn about them, and reach out to them.

What about LinkedIn for a Job Search?

Okay, we focus on B2B lead gen, but you may have friends who are looking for jobs. Much of this book will also be useful for them so we'll add a few notes here and there on using LinkedIn for a job search.

Summary

In this book, we'll look at LinkedIn with the concept of inbound and outbound marketing for lead gen.

- Inbound marketing with profiles, organization pages, posts, and articles: you'll see how to attract others
- Outbound marketing with Sales Navigator: you'll see how to find leads, learn about them, follow them, and contact them

Use Your LinkedIn Profile for Inbound Marketing

Your LinkedIn profile is how people find you, evaluate you, and choose to talk with you. All LinkedIn services are built around your profile.

In this chapter, we'll show you how to build your profile.

Your Profile

People search for the solution to their problem or concern. Your profile should show that you can solve or deal with their problem or concern.

LinkedIn gives your profile a score, based on completeness of your profile, activity, and other factors (we'll cover all of these in this book). The higher your score, the more your profile will be shown to potential business partners, recruiters, and so on. A complete profile is essential for success in LinkedIn.

Your Profile Photo

The profile photo is your face in your profile.

- Your photo should communicate how you want to be seen. People judge you by the way you present yourself. If a book's cover is 50% of the book, then your photo is 50% of your profile. It's their first impression of you.
- In general, the style of your photo should resemble the photo of others in your field. If you want to run a surfing school in Hawaii, then a snapshot on the beach is perfect. If you're

looking for positions in banking or insurance, you should look like a banker.

- Get a professional photograph.
- Don't use selfies or snapshots. Don't use photos with someone's arm draped around you or a beer bottle in your hand. Don't dress or pose in a provocative way. Don't wear sunglasses or hats.
- Show only your head and shoulders. People want to see your face and eyes.
- Use your photo in PNG format. This looks better than JPG.

Here are several examples of profile photos:

Nic Peterson leads scrum and agile workshops and from his photo, you can see he's friendly and energetic.

Roger Kuo does biz dev for large companies, so his profile photo is corporate yet relaxed.

Hope Frank's photo shows confidence and openness, which is what a top CMO should be.

Make sure your profile photo can be seen by others. In your "Me" pulldown menu of the navigation bar, find "Settings and Privacy. On the "Account tab" find "Site Preferences," and scroll down to "Showing profile photos." Make sure this is set to "Everyone."

Header Image

This is the background image in your profile that appears behind your photo. Use it to visually communicate and reinforce your services or products and how you add value. If you're a moving company, show a photo of your truck and smiling crew while moving boxes. If you're a consultant, show a professional photo of yourself.

Don't waste this space with pretty sunsets or abstract patterns. The image should show what you do. Look at others in your industry and see what they use.

The header image is 1584 pixels wide by 396 pixels high (1584x396). This is a 4:1 proportion. Use PNG image format, which is clearer than JPG format.

Be sure to check how your profile appears both on desktop and on cell phones. We've found that it's easier to adjust the layout of the header image for a cell phone.

The Headline

The headline is the caption to your photo. It fills two to three lines of text below your photo.

The headline is a short summary of what you offer to others. A good headline quickly tells people what you can do for them. This means the headline should focus on your customer's needs.

This means the caption isn't about you ("I have an MBA…"). It should offer an answer to your customer's problem or area of interest ("I build your sales pipeline.")

- Your headline caption should be customer-centric and state the benefits of your service or product to your customer
- If you're looking for a job, state what you want to do, such as "Seeking Regional Sales Manager Jobs"
- You have 120 characters so choose your words carefully.

Here are a few examples of good headlines:

- Samantha Hartley: Creator of The Path To $2M™ ♦ Helping Women Consultants Sell 6 and 7 Figure Engagements (Without Overwhelm)
- Steven Perchikov: Booking highly qualified prospects on your calendar + helping you close them.
- Blake Schofield: I help women transition from unfulfilling careers by creating a bridge to fulfillment on their terms.
- Stacy Jones: Bring the Power of Pop Culture To Your Brand
- Max Berry: I help feature your brand in Forbes, Inc, Entrepreneur, Bloomberg & others to establish massive credibility and trust.

Notice they're not selling. They're offering to help you: to get six-figure engagements, to book highly qualified prospects to your calendar, get into Forbes, and so on.

You can test headlines to find the best one. Use Google Ads (formerly called "AdWords") and create ads for yourself. Use a small budget (say, $25 and $0.50 bids), add the top 10-20 keywords for what you do, and create perhaps four or five ads. Put your headlines in the description text. The ads should have identical headings. Run these ads for two weeks (ten business days) without major holidays. Look at the click-through-rate (CTR) to pick the top two ads. Pause the other ads. Use the top two ads to write additional versions where you try different words, swap words, and so on. You'll quickly find an ad with high CTR, which you can use for your headline.

Tip: When you create a new Google Adwords account, Google gives you $100 in credit. This means you can test your ads for free.

The About Summary

The About summary is the block of text under your short headline.

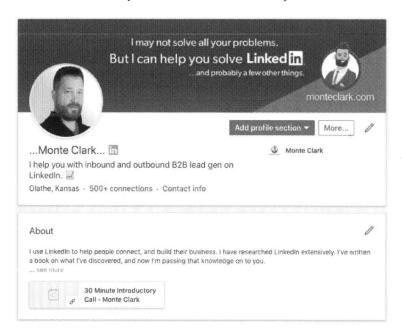

When someone comes to your profile page, they see two lines about you which ends with "Show More…" They click that to see your full summary.

It should clearly show what you can do for them. What value will you add if they connect to you?

A good method is to state a question or bold statement and follow it with your solution. The best About Us sections tell your story and give someone something to relate to. You need to quickly give someone a reason to reach out to you and get on your calendar. End it with a call-to-action. "Call me now" or "Email me."

Use bullet points to highlight specific skills, use short sentences, and put space between your paragraphs so it's easy to scan.

Experience

The experience section is what we normally put in a resume. Positions, job titles, organizations, dates (start and end), and a short summary of each position.

Your experience section should assure the visitor that you're interested and dedicated to what you do. It should indicate that you have the necessary skills, competence, capacity and reliability. Don't list irrelevant jobs or experience

For job seekers, list the skills, tools, software and technology that you use. Recruiters search for those words.

Education

List all relevant certificates, licenses, and education. LinkedIn uses this information to show profiles to people who are searching for people in that field.

LinkedIn, Google, and other search engines have access to university student databases. They can quickly verify if someone graduated in finance from Michigan State. Don't list fake diplomas or certificates.

Volunteer Experience

List your extracurricular volunteer activity here. It looks better when people see that you're active in your community. This includes Red Cross, your church, scouting, city activities, and so on.

Skills and Endorsements

People can endorse you for skills, such as finance or digital marketing. Others can add their vote to your skill, so you end up with dozens of endorsements and votes.

You can manage this list. It's better to have many votes on a few highly relevant skills than to have a few votes spread across many marginal skills.

Look at the endorsements that people have added to your profile. By deleting the irrelevant or marginal skills, you can focus people's votes on the top skills that you want show.

- Skills: List your top three skills. If other skills should be in the top three, click the little pushpin icon at the left of the skill to move it to the top. If there are already three in the top skills, click the pushpin icon to remove it from the top three so you can add a new item to the top three.

- Industry Knowledge: List of additional skills. If there are skills which overlap (such as "web analytics" and "analytics"), delete the one with less votes. You can also grab the four bars at the right and drag the skills up and down to reorder by priority.

- Tools: LinkedIn looks at your profile, notes the tools that frequently appear in your jobs, and adds some of them to this list.

To edit your skills, click the pencil icon.

Don't ask friends and family to endorse your skills. Endorsements from relevant people in your industry have more weight than random votes. LinkedIn looks at who endorse you so they can weed out the light or fake profiles.

Recommendations

Ask your managers, college instructors, and others to write recommendations for you. People read these to get a sense of who you are.

You should also write recommendations for others.

Accomplishments

You can list significant accomplishments, such as books that you've written, awards or recognitions, mountains that you've climbed, and so on.

Languages

List the languages that you speak fluently. That doesn't mean you can order at a hot dog stand! ☐ This should be languages in which you can hold a business meeting.

Interests

Finally, add your interests. These are the people, activities, and things that interest you.

- Influencers: These are leaders in your field or key people in your industry whom you follow. By listing these, others can see that you know who is important in your field.
- Companies: These are relevant companies and organization that you follow. This can include clients, companies where you've worked, and companies where you would like to work.
- Groups: These are associations, clubs, and memberships. You should list all professional societies and groups for your career.
- Schools: Universities and colleges. If you're interested in MIT and CalTech, you can enter them here and LinkedIn will show postings and articles from them.

By adding these people, companies, and groups, you show LinkedIn what interests you so LinkedIn can show relevant postings and articles to you.

When people review your profile, they will look at your interests. They will be more likely to contact you if there are common interests.

This also works in the other direction. You can use groups to find people who also like what you like. It's much easier to establish a connection if there are shared interests.

LinkedIn also uses this to establish the quality of your connections and experience in your field.

Edit Your Public Profile URL

You can change your LinkedIn URL to something that is easier to put in your business card and for people to write down. If your LinkedIn URL is something like linkedin.com/in/ 527334563454, you can change it to linkedin.com/in/laura-jones/. Monte has linkedin.com/in/MonteClark/ and Andreas has linkedin.com/in/AndreasRamos/. If the name is available, you can get it.

To change your URL:

- Click the Me icon at the top of your LinkedIn homepage
- Click View profile
- On your profile page, click Edit public profile & URL on the right
- Under Edit URL in the right rail, click the Edit icon next to your public profile URL
- It'll be an address that looks like www.linkedin.com/in/yourname
- Type the last part of your new custom URL in the text box and save

Profile Settings and Privacy

You must make sure your profile will be visible to others. If you set up LinkedIn many years ago, you may have used settings that you've forgotten. Go through your privacy settings. You find your Profile Settings and Privacy in your "Me" menu.

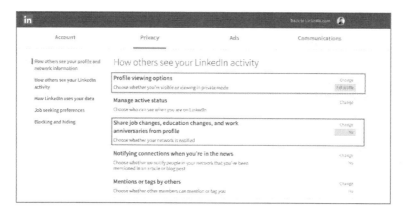

Two settings are important:

- Profile Viewing Options: You can choose whether your profile will be visible or not in LinkedIn. If you're looking for jobs or connections, this should be open.

- Sharing your profile job changes, education changes, and work anniversaries: If this is open, your connections are notified whenever you make a change to your profile, such as changes in job titles, additional certifications, birthdays, and so on. There's a reason to turn this off temporarily: while you're editing your profile, you can set this to "no" so your network doesn't get notified with every single edit. Once you are satisfied with your profile, change it so that you alert your network with changes to your profile.

Check these settings. We've looked at our clients' account and often found they had set this long ago to no-show and then wondered why nobody contacted them.

All-Star Profiles

Once you've completed all requirements, you get an All-Star badge.

The All-Star badge means your profile will show up more often in LinkedIn. So… complete your profile!

Improve Your Profile with LinkedIn Learning

Technology and information move very quickly now so you must constantly learn new skills and broaden your knowledge about your field.

Lynda.com, started by Lynda Weinman, offers thousands of online courses in many fields and software. In 2015, LinkedIn bought Lynda.com for $1.5 billion. You can use Lynda.com to learn just about any software, marketing, or sales techniques for only $25 per month.

Go to the "Work" icon in your navigation bar at the top of your LinkedIn home page. Click the icon and look for the Learning button.

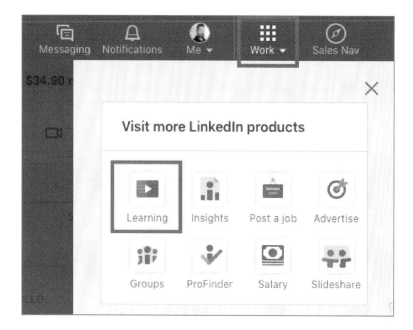

Once you've selected the learning section, you can search the courses:

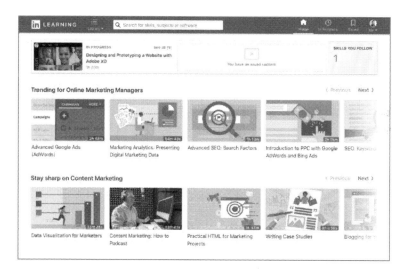

When you've completed a course, it may show up on your LinkedIn account as an accomplishment. The more accomplishments you have, the higher your score in LinkedIn.

Here's an example of courses that Monte took at LinkedIn:

LinkedIn recommends courses to you based on your profile and background. For example, if you're in business development, you will find courses on sales technique, business development, and so on.

Tip: Over 120,000 public libraries offer free access to Lynda.com courses. Check with your public library.

Use LinkedIn to Find a Job

Okay, we're realistic: many people will use LinkedIn only to find a job. Let's add a few notes on job seeking with LinkedIn.

For a long time, LinkedIn was pretty much a resume database for recruiters. People posted their resumes and both internal and external recruiters used LinkedIn to find candidates.

- An internal recruiter is a recruiter who works in a organization's human resources (HR) department and looks for workers. These mid-level recruiters use LinkedIn to find people who are looking for work or staffers who may want to switch.

- An external recruiter works for a recruiting agency. The agency is hired by companies to find people. External recruiters work at several layers: at the low end, they supply temporary staffers. Other recruiters place staffers for one or two years. At the high end, executive recruiters look for candidates are already working at other companies and approach them to see if they'll quit and join the company. These external recruiters are also called headhunters. External recruiters look at a company's competitors to see whom they can poach. They also look at LinkedIn to learn about the potential target.

All these recruiters use a recruiter's version of LinkedIn to search, sort, and evaluate resumes.

Be sure to write your profile so it's easy for LinkedIn's recruiter software to find and rank your resume.

- Use the top keywords and phrases for your field and industry. Make sure these keywords are close together. The recruiter tools look for proximity of keywords. This means when the recruiter searches for Python, banking software, transactions, and Oracle database, the resumes where these words are clustered together will rank higher.

- Don't use vague descriptions such as "large company", "regional sales", or "well-known clients". Nobody searches for that. Be specific. You worked at General Motors. You were the top salesperson in 2018 for California. Your clients included Citibank, Chase Manhattan, and Wells-Fargo.
- Businesses post their jobs in LinkedIn. Find companies where you would like to work and go to their business page. Learn about the company and see if you have connections to people who already work at the company. In interviews, let them know that you researched the company.

You must also do all the steps we outlined for improving your profile. Get a professional photograph. Write a good summary. Your resume is scored on activity, so be active in LinkedIn. Use LinkedIn to request recommendations from your college professors, instructors, and managers. Post to LinkedIn and engage with postings. Use the training courses at LinkedIn to learn more skills. Your score will go up and you'll appear in more recruiters' searches.

Tip: The recruiter resume search tools also score you on freshness. They prefer a resume that was posted recently instead of a resume from two years ago. Recruiters get to their desks on Monday morning and start searching. So... on Sunday night, you go to your LinkedIn profile and swap two words around. Take the phrase "Skills include database, sales, negotiation" and change it to "Skills include database, negotiation, sales". Just swap two words and save. Your resume is now fresh and will show up on Monday morning.

Use Your LinkedIn QR Code on Your Phone

LinkedIn gives you a QR code that points to your profile.

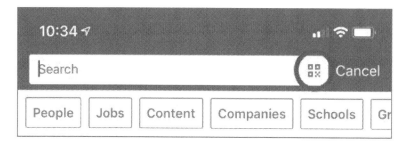

To get your own QR code:

- Download, install, and open the LinkedIn app
- In the Search bar at the top of the LinkedIn app, tap the QR icon
- Tap the My Code button to get your QR code

To scan someone's QR code:

- Open the LinkedIn app on your mobile device
- In the Search bar at the top of the LinkedIn app, tap the QR icon
- Tap the Scan button
- The person's LinkedIn profile will open

You can use your QR codes on your business card, your PowerPoint presentations, articles, flyers, brochures, books, advertising, and so on. A clever idea is to save your QR code in your phone's photo gallery. When someone wants to link to you, you can show them your QR code, they can scan it with their phone, and you're connected.

Here are the QR codes for Monte and Andreas. Go ahead and try to scan these with your phone.

Who Has Viewed Your Profile

Under your profile, there is Your Dashboard, which shows data about your profile.

Click on "Who viewed your profile" to see who has viewed your profile for the last ninety days. You can see where your searchers work, what they do at their work, and what keywords they used to find you. If they're a potential lead for business, you can connect with them and following their content.

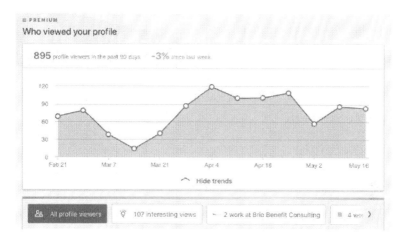

At the right of Your Dashboard, there is Search Appearances. Click that to see:

- Where they work
- What they do (by job title)
- Keywords your searchers used

Look at the last one carefully. These are the words that people use to find you. If these words matter to you, be sure to use them in your profile heading, description, and job descriptions.

A Final Note about Your Presence Offline versus Online

The online world has become such a big part of our current world that many forget the offline world.

This is especially true with social media influencers who amass millions of followers, become celebrities, and often wealthy as well. Why work (or even go to university?) if you can just jump around in the surf and make hundreds of thousands of dollars every month?

An online presence, counted in impressions, followers, and endorsement fees, is great for social media, but there is little reality to it. Digital celebrity lasts only a few years and then what? What kind of job is there for a used-to-be-a-celebrity?

In the real world, we have to build up our personal connections for a decade or two until we become sufficiently established in the business world or academia. Professional presence is based on real achievements, such as university degrees, credentials, professional licenses, and certifications. Careers last decades. All of these are difficult to establish and expensive to maintain, and that's precisely the point: it weeds out the wannabes. Only the hard core keeps at it over the long term.

It's easy to create fake profiles on the web. You can buy fake diplomas from top universities and pad your resume with non-existent job titles and experience. This fraud is wide spread in Facebook, Instagram, Twitter, and even Google search results because those companies don't care much about what you do.

But LinkedIn is different. Because LinkedIn wants to be the social network of professional people, it blocks fake credentials. As you've seen, articles are reviewed by people at LinkedIn to see if it's useful or just spam. LinkedIn uses software to identify and remove fake profiles.

Your Profile in Another Language

You can add a profile in another language:

- Click the Me icon at top of your LinkedIn homepage
- Click View profile
- Click Add profile in another language at the right
- Choose a language in the dropdown list
- Update your name if it's different in another language (for example, Chinese, Japanese, or Arabic)
- Add your headline. You have only 120 characters, including spaces.
- Click Create Profile.

You can add several more languages.

Is this necessary? English is the universal language for business, finance, and technology, so it's good enough for most people. If you work with China or the Arab world, it may help.

Don't use Google Translate. A bad translation is worse than no translation. If you use Chinese, make sure it's correct Chinese.

Summary

To use Inbound marketing, you make a strong offer that attracts visitors. They are looking for solutions to their problems. When people search, your profile should show up in the list of results, and they should see at a glance that you have what they want.

Build your LinkedIn profile for this purpose. It's not a job resume nor a list of all of your skills. Your profile should appeal to your target audience.

Use Your Company Pages for Inbound Marketing

Company pages are miniature websites. You tell your story, post available jobs, highlight what you are doing, talk about team members, and offer a corporate blog. If you have a blog on your website, copy it and post to LinkedIn.

Your business should have a company page on LinkedIn. There are four reasons:

- Verification: People will research you and your company before they contact you. A company page shows them what your company does, along with full contact information, including your website address. Company pages also show who works for your company and job openings. People can follow your company page. Whenever you post to your company page, your followers will see your postings.

- Search results: LinkedIn shows your company page in their search results. People can search by company name, keywords, or #hashtags. Use basic SEO (search engine optimization) to write a description of your company with the best keywords and #hashtags so people can find you and your company.

- Hiring: You can post job openings on your company page. These job postings are better than job postings at recruiter sites or job sites because the company avoids recruiter fees. Those fees can be 20-30% and guess who pays the fee? The worker. If a company is willing to pay $100,000 for a staff positions, the candidates who apply through the company's page will get $100,000, but staffers who apply through job staffing companies will get $70,000. The recruiting company takes its share. These workers discover they're underpaid, and they may quit. It's better for the company to hire directly instead of through recruiters.

- Employee Engagement: You should encourage employees to engage with content that's posted to the company page. When content is posted, followers, including employees, get a notice. They should add their comments and share the post to their personal feed. The more activity on a posting, the more it will be distributed by LinkedIn.

Setting Up a Company Page

You set up a company page in the same way you create your profile page. Show what you do for your customer, explain how you can help clients, and offer useful information.

To create your company page, click your "Me" navigation at the top of the page and select "Create Company Page."

Animate Your Company Page Icon

You can animate your company page icon. Any graphics artist can turn your organization's icon into an animated GIF. See an example at linkedin.com/company/grant-thornton-llp/

Personal Profile or Company Page?

Some companies like to think they're more important than their staff. But companies don't matter very much and that's obvious when you think about it. You deal with companies only when you buy a Big Mac or rent a car: These companies don't personally know you and the worker behind the desk has no say in the matter. Just try negotiating a better price on your next Big Mac! That'll be a funny video for Youtube.

The B2B world is made of social networks of personal relationships, based on professionalism, common interests, shared experience, common values, and trust. All of LinkedIn's features, including training, salary information, groups, the tools for recruiters, Sales Navigator, and so on are all focused on people.

Look at your profile page and work on it. It's not easy: we find it takes two to three weeks to create a good profile page.

By the way, we interviewed a friend for this book who was using LinkedIn for her job search. A recruiter said to her, "It's not very important to be active on LinkedIn. If we hire you, we'll need you to cancel your account." Well! This company wants to make sure their employees can't be found by other companies, presumably to trap them or diminish their marketability. This let her know the company was not for her.

Your Company Page Is a Team Page

Jason McDonald writes in *The Social Media Marketing Workbook* that company pages should be a team sport. That's the best way to think about company pages. Just as the US women's soccer team depends on all players in the team, not just the top players, a company page is successful when everyone plays the game.

Every employee must have a complete profile in LinkedIn. This broadens the team's overall exposure in LinkedIn because this will offer many points of contact: several dozen universities, hundreds of previous companies and jobs, hundreds of interests, and so on. Your company should help staff to improve their LinkedIn profiles. Don't do this for just the top four or five people in your company. All employees should have complete profiles.

But just standing on the field isn't enough; the soccer team must kick the ball. LinkedIn also keeps track of activity. Everyone should be active on LinkedIn. They should follow each other and when they see a posting or article, they should engage with it. The more engagement, the more distribution and visibility.

Everyone should use the company's top keywords. The social media team should make a list of five to ten top keywords and #hashtags and distribute this. They should also work with staff to show them how to use #hashtags and @mentions. This may sound obvious to you, but most of the people with whom we talk about LinkedIn don't know how to use these.

LinkedIn Search and EAT: Expertise, Authority, Trust

Let's step into the world of SEO for a moment. SEO is Search Engine Optimization, which is the method of getting websites to show up higher in Google. To do that, it helps to understand how Google ranks web pages in the search results.

Google uses three criteria: expertise, authority, and trust (their acronym is "E.A.T.") as a major factor in their ranking algorithm. They look for the websites and pages that show:

- Expertise: The author of the page is an expert on the topic
- Authority: The author of the page is seen as an authority on the topic by other known authorities on the same topic
- Trust: The author of the page is seen as trustworthy, in contrast to scam and fraud pages which are untrustworthy

This means the Google search engine algorithm isn't just a question of keywords and links. Google looks at off-page factors, such as credentials (certificates, diploma, license, and so on), position and activity within professional organizations, and so on. Google developed this as a result of the never-ending work to block spammers, irrelevant items, and fraud. All search engines, including Google, Microsoft Bing, Baidu, and Yandex, use a form of EAT.

LinkedIn is also a sort of search engine. Google indexes, ranks, and displays pages, which are sorted by value. LinkedIn does the same, but instead of websites, it ranks and displays people.

LinkedIn wants to offer the best possible profile, company, and content for a search. Since there is opportunity to make lots of money in LinkedIn, scammers also try to show up. To block that, LinkedIn has a large team to identify and block spammers.

LinkedIn looks at your connections, credentials (certificates, diploma, and so on), activity, interests, and background, such as the companies where you've worked. Successful people have similar track records of long history in the same industry with ever-increase responsibility and job titles. They also have connections from others in their industry, along with recommendations.

That's why you should have a complete profile in LinkedIn.

Summary of Your Profile

As we've learned while writing this book and talking with dozens of people, most people don't understand what LinkedIn means to their career. In general, profiles are poorly done, with random snapshot photos, weak descriptions, just a few jobs, and so on. That doesn't say much about the person. Or perhaps it says too much: when you see a weak LinkedIn profile, it tells you the person isn't very serious about his career.

That's why we put this effort into writing about your profile page. LinkedIn evaluates people by the profile. A good profile page will be shown to other people; a weak profile page won't show up because others don't want to see connections to individuals with weak profiles.

Use Your Connections for Inbound Marketing

Your Network Reflects You

LinkedIn looks at the quality of your connections to get a better picture of you. The quality of your network reflects on you. As the French say, "If I know your friends, I know you."

Use Advanced Search to Find Connections

You can use LinkedIn's advanced search to find people for connections.

To use Advanced Search, select "people" under the search window and then click the "All Filters" menu.

This brings up a set of filters.

In Advanced Search, you can narrow your search by selecting and combining queries, such as:

- Connections of an existing connection
- Countries, states, provinces, cities
- Company (even if there isn't a company page on LinkedIn)
- Industries
- Languages
- Schools
- Interests and keywords
- Name of a person including their title, company, and school

How to Write an Introduction Message

When you ask to connect to someone, you should include a personal message. Show that you have a mutual interest. This gives them a reason to accept your request. Some ideas include:

- Interests (We both work in aeronautic engineering)
- Job history (We both worked at IBM)
- Education (We both went to University of Chicago)
- Location (We both live in Paris)

Read the person's profile and write a short meaningful introduction to improve your connection rate. Start by showing interest in talking with them. Here are a few examples:

- Hello, John, I see you're from Houston. We often travel to Houston and love the city!
- Hello, Laura, I was looking at your profile and see you completed the LinkedIn Marketing Technology course. I was considering that course. Did you think it's worthwhile?

The second step is to give a reason for the connection. Write a short sentence to say why you would like to connect with them.

- I'm interested in connecting because we both work in blockchain banking.
- I see that your specialty is in search engine optimization. I'd like to hear your thoughts.

Show the person that you've read her posts, articles, or books.

- I saw your post about blockchain economics and wrote a comment
- Re-share a post and use the "@mention" so they know you have shared their content
- When you use an @mention, the person is notified
- When the post appears, the person's name is a clickable link

People will notice when you engage with their postings and articles. They'll pay attention to you.

Close the message with an action step. Ask the person to connect with you. This can be a simple "Would you consider connecting to me?"

You will have a good chance of a connection when you learn about the person, give a reason for the connection, and invite them to connect.

You can also simply connect to people without an introduction message. If you have a good photo and description, they may accept.

Send Messages and InMail

There are two types of messages in LinkedIn: Messages and InMail:

- You can send a message to anyone if both of you are connected. Click Messages and write your message. Regrettably, LinkedIn's message tool is very simple.

- When you pay for Premium or Sales Navigator, you can send InMail. This lets you send a message to anyone, even if you don't have a connection to the person.

- Don't spam people with offers or attempts to sell. They can easily click Report button and mark you as a spammer. LinkedIn will look at the person's messages and if he is abusing the system, they'll block the account.

Should You Accept or Reject Connections?

Why accept connections from anyone?

Some people accept anyone who requests a connection (they're called "open network people"). Monte and Andreas accept all connection requests (LinkedIn.com/in/MonteClark and LinkedIn.com/in/AndreasRamos). But don't spam; we'll block you!

We recommend you should also accept all connections. Here are several reasons for this:

- You may think a connection has little value now, but what about the future? The student who asks for a connection today may start the next Google.
- You don't know the other person's connections. It's possible she may be connected to someone else who can be a good connection for you.
- The more connections you have, the greater your reach to first-, second-, and third-level connections
- The more connections you have, the more people who will see your profile, postings, and articles

You can always remove connections. If someone connects to you and then spams you, you can block them.

 Connections (2,161)

 Groups (5)

 Companies (15)

Hashtags (5)

Add personal contacts

We'll periodically import and store your contacts to help you and others connect. You choose who to connect to and who to invite. **Learn more**

Continue

More options

The Limits on Connections

You can have up to 30,000 LinkedIn connections. It's the same whether you invite them, or they request a connection. When you reach the limit and you want to add another, you must delete a previous connection. So... go ahead and invite the first 25,000 but be careful with the last few thousand invites.

In the beginning, there was no limit and some of the early birds have 100,000 or more connections. In a way, the number doesn't matter much. You should have many, but when you get past 10,000, your second tier and third-tier connections will be pretty much everyone who is relevant to you.

To see your number of connections, click on My Network. At the left, you'll see Connections and a number.

Regrettably, there's no easy way to delete connections. You select them, one by one. We gave up on trying to remove connections.

Your Join-Date and Member Number

You can see when you joined LinkedIn and your member number.
1. Click your photo at the top of LinkedIn to open your settings
2. Select Settings & Privacy
3. The day you joined is at the top of the page

Here is Andreas' join date:

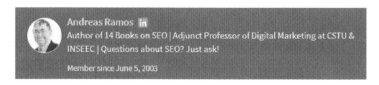

LinkedIn opened on Dec. 28, 2002, so he joined within the first six months.

What about his member number?

1. Open your profile page
2. In a blank area in your profile, right-click and select View Source
3. This opens the HTML code for your page
4. Use search (Control + F) and search for "member"
5. This finds your member number in the code.

Here is Andreas' member number:

```
iac.web.extended.close-colleagues-m
quot;urn:li:member:6701&quot;},&quo
t;voyager.mynetwork.web.customize-a
ot;voyager.mynetwork.web.customize-
```

Andreas' number is 6701. When LinkedIn started, they wanted to look bigger, so the number started at 1,000. This means Andreas was #5701. By the way, you can only see your number, but not anyone else.

Does this mean anything? No. But it's kinda interesting.

Summary

There is widespread misinformation about LinkedIn connections. Many people refuse to add connections, so they only have a few. You should add connections who are relevant to your field, active in your field, and, if it matters, in your geographical location (country, city, and so on). This increases your relevance in LinkedIn, which makes it easier for others to find you. Use LinkedIn filters to find people and send connection requests. Add a short note to show why a connection will be useful.

Use Posts and Articles for Inbound Marketing

LinkedIn isn't just for business networking. It's also a publishing platform.

Content marketing started in 2009 and has become a major form of marketing because people share useful information with their friends, family, coworkers and potential customers. Therefore, LinkedIn has tools to let you publish and share information.

There are two forms of content: short posts and long articles. Let's look at each of these.

Posts

Posts are what you see in the newsfeed of your main page. Your posts are shown to your connections in their news feed.

- Posts are short items with a combination of words, illustration, video, and attachments (such as PDFs, Word documents, or spreadsheets)
- Ideas for posts include company news, events, activities, promotions, projects, successes, new team members, industry insights, philanthropic activity, white paper material, case studies and so on. You can also say that you're hiring
- You can add #hashtags to your posting.
- The limit is 1300 characters, or about two short paragraphs

Articles

Just as you post articles to your blog, you can post articles to LinkedIn. LinkedIn articles has several advantages:

- Large audience: Over 645 million LinkedIn (July 2019) members so your article can get wider readership
- Review: A LinkedIn team reviews every article to make sure it's appropriate. They block spam, irrelevant items, and fraud. This ensures the quality of articles.
- Promotion: LinkedIn will push your article to relevant audiences. If you write about aerodynamics, it will be shown to people who are interested in aerodynamics. This also means LinkedIn doesn't annoy people by showing irrelevant articles.
- Google's respect: Because LinkedIn moderates articles, Google gives greater weight to LinkedIn articles. These show higher in Google search results.
- Your profile: Articles become part of your profile and are listed in your profile's Articles section
- Follows: People can click Follow on your article to follow you without becoming connected to you

Not all accounts have permission to publish articles. To see if you have permission, go to your News feed. At the top, under "Start a Post", you may have "Write an Article". The higher your score and the more active you are, the better the chance to get permission to write articles.

Articles can include text, images, and video. You can also use #hashtags in articles.

When your article appears, you can get its link and post it in your Twitter account, create Google Ads for it, email it to others, and so on.

You can also search for articles in LinkedIn. You can use Google and search for <site:linkedin.com/pulse {keyword}>, such as <site:linkedin.com/pulse aerodynamics>.

By the way, LinkedIn Articles used to be called LinkedIn Pulse, so you may occasionally still see that name.

What to Post

- Postings and articles should have value, such as ideas, information, and similar
- Be relevant to your industry
- Be credible and trustworthy
- LinkedIn also prefers content that is exclusive to LinkedIn
- Keep your content simple. Most LinkedIn members aren't native speakers of English. Keep sentences short and use clear grammar.

What You Should Not Post

If someone breaks LinkedIn's posting policies, they will limit, suspend, or close the account. Here are some of the rules at LinkedIn:

- Don't advertise or promote. If you want to advertise, use LinkedIn ads or contact LinkedIn Marketing Solutions.
- Don't violate copyrights. You must have permission to share or publish. This may include content that belongs to your employer.
- Don't post anything that can be misleading, fraudulent, obscene, threatening, hateful, defamatory, discriminatory, or illegal.

You can find this and more at http://bit.ly/30jn55i

How Often Should You Post?

The more engagement with your post, the higher your score at LinkedIn. This includes the number of likes, views, comments, shares, time viewed, the acceleration of activity, and other factors. The higher your score, the more distribution for your posts and articles.

Add Images and Video to Your Posts

Any post or article gets more attention if it has photographs, tables, graphs, or videos. Regrettably, LinkedIn doesn't accept animated gifs (for now...)

- For posts, images should be 552 (w) x 276 (h) pixels in png or jpg format (png is better)

- For articles, the cover photo should be 2000 (w) x 600 (h) pixels and images should be 744 (w) X 400 (h) pixels in png or jpg format (png is better)

- Video is better than photos. You can use your cell phone to do interviews or video of yourself. Keep videos to two-to-four minutes and state clearly at the beginning what you will say. Add subtitles to your video. Many people use LinkedIn at work, so they often won't use sound.

You should check your image's width because LinkedIn will shrink or stretch your image to fit the space, which may distort the image.

- If you use images that were made by others, make sure you have written permission.

- You can get copyright-free images at PixaBay, Pexels, Unsplash, Burst, PicJumbo, and more

- To add an image, click the little camera icon

- To add video, click the video camera icon

Engaging with Posts and Articles by Others

Engaging with your connections' posts and articles is equally important. When you play catch with your friends, but you only throw the ball, the game won't last very long. There are reasons for engaging with others:

- It shows you're listening to them
- By commenting instead of simply liking a post, you give them an opportunity to respond
- They may also look at your posts and articles
- Engagement by you to others' postings also improves your score. The higher your score, your profile will appear more often and higher in searches.

Use Posts and Articles to Find People

Another way to find people is to look for posts and articles on a topic. Find articles and then look at the person who wrote it.

To do this:

- Use Search and search for a keyword, such as "aerodynamic engineering".
- Click on Content to see articles about that keyword
- Note who is posting the article
- If it's relevant, connect to them

LinkedIn's Algorithm for Posts and Articles

Most platforms such as Google, Facebook, and Instagram don't explain how they work. LinkedIn is open and explains their algorithm and ranking process. Some of the criteria include:

- LinkedIn gives weight to posts and articles shared by your connections, job recommendations that are relevant to your job title and skills, news recommendations, suggestions for connection to other members ("People You May Know"), news stories mentioning companies that you or your connections are following, and similar. The goal is to offer timely and relevant information.

- Weight is given to posts and articles that get engagement and interaction, such clicks, likes, comments, shares, time viewed, and so on
- Weight is also given to the quality and level of completion of profiles. Low-quality members generally have light profiles, few skills, and many sections are blank. Since people with extensive experience and skills are more likely to be valuable connections to you, LinkedIn gives preference to better profiles. This is another reason why you should make sure your profile is as good as possible.

The name at LinkedIn for this activity on your posts and articles is *decoration*. The more decoration, the higher your post will rank.

LinkedIn's algorithm ranks and distributes your posts in several steps:

- The first pass, named First Pass Rankers (FPRs), creates a ranking based on relevance to you. This includes jobs recommendations, news, posts, and articles, updates or shares from your connections, suggestions for new connections from LinkedIn (which is called "People You May Know" (PYMK), and sponsored updates (SUs) (the advertising).
- FPR results goes to the Second Pass Ranker (SPR) that combines all the FPRs to create a single personalized ranked list for you.
- This finally goes to a reranking stage which adjusts the SPR to create the final feed to you.

This is described at http://bit.ly/2Yu5C8e

Here is LinkedIn's diagram of their filter algorithm:

There are four stages to the LinkedIn algorithm:

- Stage #1, Machine Learning: LinkedIn uses filters and software to check if the material is spam, irrelevant, or violates any policy. If it violates a policy, the item is blocked. If there is doubt, the item is sent to human reviewers to see if the content is acceptable or not. If someone violates LinkedIn rules, their account is flagged.

- Stage #2, Feed Test: Your posting appears in the news feed. If the posting or article quickly gets engagement (Likes, comments, and reposts), then the article gets more distribution. Comments and reposts have a higher value than Likes.

- The time of posting is important because you need decoration as quickly as possible. You should post when your audience is online. We'll cover that later in this book.

- Stage #3, Network Test: Your post is compared to part of your connections. If you get decoration, your post appears to yet more connections. When there is no further engagement, your post disappears.
- Stage #4, People Test: Your post is finally reviewed by a person at LinkedIn. They evaluate whether your post should continue to appear, be distributed to a different channel, and what, if anything, LinkedIn can learn from your post to further train the algorithm.

If someone want to reach people in aerodynamics, then they need connections to people in aerodynamics. That also means a person's social network acts as a group filter: if the aerodynamics community doesn't engage with someone's postings, it signals the person's postings are irrelevant. Connect to as many people in your field as possible and offer high-quality postings and articles to your field.

You can see who is looking at your profile and postings:

1. Find relevant connections. Go to the Home page. At the left side, under your photo, click on "Who's Viewed Your Profile" and the number.
2. Under the graph, click the button "15 Interesting Views". These people are highly relevant to you.
3. Review the list of people.
4. If they're already connected to you, can click "Message" and write to them
5. If they're not connected, click "Connect" and write a short message to them.

There are several ways to see who is engaging with your postings

1. At the top of your LinkedIn homepage, click the Me icon, click Manage, and click Posts & Activity
2. Under each post or article, you can see the number of likes and comments
3. You can also the number of views for your post in the News feed
4. As you improve your profile and connections, the number of views will increase

You can improve your engagement by posting when your audience is online. To find time and location of your audience, go to Google Analytics for your website and select Audience | Geo | Location.

Let's look at the data for Andreas' website. Google Analytics shows that most of his traffic is in the United States, so we click on the United States in the map to get the following table:

Region	Acquisition			Behavior			
	Users	New Users	Sessions	Bounce Rate	Pages / Session	Avg. Session Duration
	30,792 % of Total: 58.70% (52,454)	30,913 % of Total: 58.66% (52,740)	41,507 % of Total: 63.01% (65,877)	74.84% Avg for View: 79.25% (-5.56%)	1.64 Avg for View: 1.49 (9.72%)	00:01:07 Avg for View: 00:00:52 (27.60%)
1. California	18,685 (59.69%)	18,536 (59.96%)	27,000 (65.05%)	72.50%	1.71	00:01:14
2. New York	1,273 (4.07%)	1,243 (4.01%)	1,477 (3.56%)	74.54%	1.67	00:01:12
3. Texas	994 (3.18%)	977 (3.16%)	1,170 (2.82%)	82.05%	1.37	00:00:41
4. Florida	664 (2.12%)	652 (2.11%)	756 (1.82%)	79.76%	1.44	00:01:04
5. Illinois	612 (1.96%)	593 (1.92%)	731 (1.76%)	74.28%	1.74	00:01:09
6. Virginia	553 (1.77%)	545 (1.76%)	618 (1.49%)	82.04%	1.41	00:00:52
7. Massachusetts	548 (1.75%)	539 (1.74%)	643 (1.55%)	75.43%	1.61	00:01:11
8. Washington	544 (1.74%)	533 (1.72%)	634 (1.53%)	79.50%	1.58	00:00:55
9. Oregon	509 (1.63%)	503 (1.63%)	573 (1.38%)	83.42%	1.32	00:00:42
10. Georgia	486 (1.55%)	484 (1.57%)	554 (1.33%)	83.03%	1.41	00:00:45

We can see at a glance that 59.7% of visitors to Andreas' website are in California. We could add Oregon and Washington state for an additional 3.1% in traffic.

What days and time of day should he post? Go to Google Analytics, click Home, and in the report, you find the following graph:

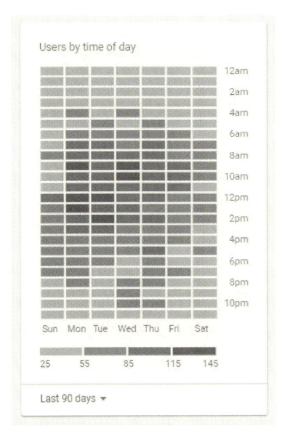

This shows you the day of the week and time of day for traffic to andreas.com. First, look at the day of the week at the bottom. Most of the traffic starts on Mondays and continues to Wednesday.

What about time of day? Are they early birds, the lunch crowd, or late afternoon coffee break? The vertical axis shows the hour of day. The darker the color, the more traffic. We can see most of his audience visits the site between 9 a.m. and 1 p.m. Pacific Standard Time (PST).

When we put together this data, we know most of his audience is in California and they're mostly online on Mondays, Tuesdays, and Wednesdays between 9 a.m. and 1 p.m. PST. He should post to LinkedIn during those times to get the most engagement and decoration.

Here's another way to find the best hour for your article.
1. Go to Google Analytics
2. Select Audience | Overview
3. Set your calendar to a business week (Monday to Friday) without major holidays before or after
4. In the resulting graph, click Hourly to see your traffic by hour of day

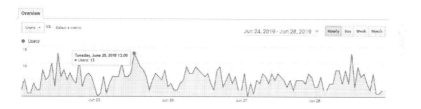

You can mouse over the graph to see the data by hour for each day of the week. In the example above, we see traffic peaked Tuesday at 1 p.m. The three spikes across the week in that graph are all 12 noon and 1 p.m.

Regrettably, there isn't similar data at LinkedIn. Some could argue that visits to a website aren't the same as visits to LinkedIn, but this is the best data that we can get, and until there is a better way, we can use this.

You should do the same analysis if you're in Canada which also spans many time zones. Europe, China, and so on have only one time zone which makes things easier. You only have to look at your country and use Google Analytics to look at the time of day for your audience.

This means if you want to reach an audience in another country, you have to consider the time and day in that country.

How to Schedule Your Posts

LinkedIn doesn't have a calendar scheduling tool for posts.

Monte uses a spreadsheet to write his posts. He makes a tab for each month and adds the workweeks and days in rows. As he finds content that he wants to forward, he copies the link to the spreadsheet.

LinkedIn allows 1,300 characters per post. You can use the Excel spreadsheet formula to count characters. For example, in cell A2, insert the formula =SUM((LEN(A1))) (where A1 is the ID of the cell with content). He also uses Grammarly to check spelling and grammar.

Monte uses his spreadsheet to keep a log of his post analytics. LinkedIn shows your posts and the data for only the last 30 days. After that, you lose both the post and the data. Currently, you need to manually keep track of what you've posted and the data so you can see what works and what doesn't.

You can use automation tools to publish to LinkedIn, such as Hootsuite, SEMRush, Postcron, Buffer, Sprout Social, MeetEdgar, and Agorapulse. But it's better to do it by hand because you can adjust the layout and so on.

Although it's manual work, you can see how the article or post will appear before you publish, and you can make any adjustments or corrections.

Views of a Posting

At the bottom of a post, you can see your post's activity and statistics.

In this example, you see Monte's post received 93 comments and 125 likes. Monte's post was seen 13,029 times in the feed.

If you get good engagement in one industry but you want more engagement in another, you can add connections in that industry. For example, if you want to get more engagement in the wine industry, add connections who work in wine.

Use #Hashtags

#Hashtags started in Twitter and spread to all other social media platforms, including LinkedIn. Google also indexes #hashtags.

- Add relevant #hashtags to your posts whenever possible
- #Hashtags are clickable. When you use a #hashtag in your posting or article, others see the #hashtag and they can click it to find additional posts and articles. That click counts as engagement for you.
- You can use #hashtags within the posting or put them at the end of your posting
- You can follow #hashtags. When postings or articles appear with those #hashtags, they'll be shown to you.
- As you write your post, LinkedIn may suggest #hashtags
- When you use #hashtags, your postings and articles will be shown to people outside your network who use or follow those #hashtags
- LinkedIn recommends not more than three #hashtags in a post
- Don't repeat hashtags in a post. LinkedIn may see this as spam and limit your views.

Here's a tip on how to find #hashtags in LinkedIn. In the LinkedIn search bar, type "#" and type your keyword slowly. As you type, LinkedIn will suggest keywords.

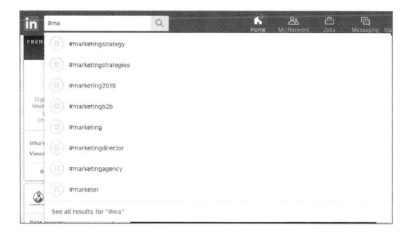

Click one (such as #marketingstrategy) and in the following screen, LinkedIn will show you how many people follow that #hashtag. #marketingstrategy. In contrast, #marketers has only 272 followers. If you use #marketingstrategy, you'll reach more marketing people. By the way, capitalize your #hashtags. It's easier to read #MarketingStrategy.

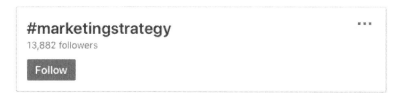

By using high-volume #hashtags, your postings will be seen by more people, which increases your visibility.

In the #hashtag search result, click the three dots in the upper right.

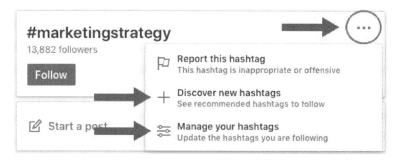

The three dots reveal a menu where you can report a #hashtag, discover new #hashtags, and manage your followed #hashtags.

Click on Discover New Hashtags to see a list of 100 #hashtags and their followers.

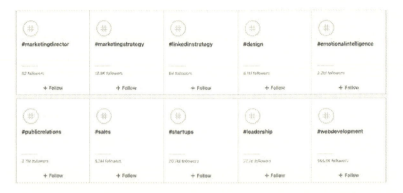

Any #hashtags you find from this list, add to your spreadsheet. You can click any of these #hashtags to get more suggestions.

Tip: Put #hashtags in context within your posting, not a list at the end, such as "I've been thinking about how to apply #MachineLearning to #MarketingStrategy and what that would look like."

Tip: When you're reading the news postings at LinkedIn, you can skip ahead. Press Control + F (find) and search (for example, marketing) and it will find hashtags that include marketing.

Use @Mentions

In LinkedIn posts, you can use a member's name to create a link to that person. The person is also notified that you used his name. These are called @mention (at-mentions).

1. Start a LinkedIn post
2. When you want to use a person's name, enter the @ symbol and then type the person's LinkedIn name. For example, Andreas types "We went bass fishing this weekend with @mo ...".
3. When he types the "@ mo...", a LinkedIn dropdown list shows first- and second-degree members in his network, along with companies where the names start with "mo..."
4. Andreas picks the one he wants (Monte Clark)
5. LinkedIn converts "@monteclark" to **Monte Clark** (in bold)
6. Monte's name (**Monte Clark**) is clickable in the post
7. Monte also gets a message that Andreas used his name

Here's an example of using an @mention in a post:

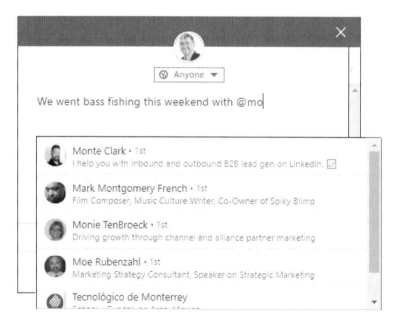

The Best Posts

Let's summarize the best posts:

- Your posts should be the kind of content that your audience wants to see at that point in their career. If your audience is made mostly young people who are starting their careers, you should post tips on how to find jobs. If your audience is established in their careers, write posts about news and developments in your industry.

- Posts should be EAT (expert, authoritative, and trustworthy). Use tips, opinions, videos, images, quotes, and links to authoritative sources.

- 60% of visits to LinkedIn are via mobile phones, so LinkedIn gives preference to posts that work well on mobile screens, which means your posts should be short, interesting, and have strong images.

- You should post on the day and hour when your audience is online.

Comment Pods

As you can see, there are many things that you can do to increase decoration: a posting should be relevant, it should be useful information, it should have photos, graphs, tables, or video, and it should be posted on the best day and time for your audience.

There's something else that you can do to boost the decoration. You can set up your own teams to add decoration to your posts.

You may have noticed that some politicians, athletes, and celebrities bring office staffers or hired temporary workers to an event. When the person speaks, the team applauds and cheers. These are called *applause teams* in politics and entertainment. At LinkedIn, these are called *comment pods*.

There are two kinds of comment pods at LinkedIn:

- Mutual comment pods are groups of like-minded friends who help to boost each other's decoration
- Organization comment pods are made of people within an organization, such as your social media marketing team

Comment pods engage with each other's posts:

- Create a private LinkedIn group
- Invite ten to twelve people
- When one of you publishes a post or article, use the group's messaging to notify the group
- Pod members see the message and they view, comment, and forward the post
- The pod's team manager makes sure all pod members are engaging with the posts
- If a post receives 20 or more comments in the first hour, views may increase by 500%.

Pods are generally about a dozen people. If it's more than that, the messages and commenting can become too much.

Your project team is a perfect group for a pod. They share the same interest in your company (you hope they do!).

Their activity has more impact when they have good profiles with lots of relevant connections, so part of the work is to improve each member's profile.

This may seem like gaming the system, but LinkedIn encouraged us to do this. Monte noticed his posts had low views, so he talked with LinkedIn customer support. They said he needed to get more comments on his posts, which he could do by setting up his comment pod.

When you use comment pod, you may get a dramatic increase in views. Monte now regularly gets 10,000 views for his postings.

But remember, it's a question of quality and relevance. If someone posts junk, LinkedIn's filters will block it (and possibly delete their account), no matter how active the pod. Write good stuff and get your pod to add applause.

Tip: When you write good articles and use comment pods to jumpstart the engagement, you can get very wide distribution to your network plus other audiences… and it's free.

About Pods

Okay, the idea of pods raises many questions. Isn't the use of pods a way of gaming the system? Yes, but LinkedIn is okay with this and there are several reasons for that.

- Can someone publish junk and use pods to get lots of views? No. Remember the diagram of LinkedIn's algorithm? The machine learning filter reviews the post for spam words. If it's spammy, it's deleted. When the post starts to grow (it gets likes, comments, and so on), it's sent to review by people at LinkedIn. If it's junk content (buy now, low quality, and so on), the post is deleted, no matter how much decoration it gets. The person who posted is flagged for review: his previous posts are reviewed; his future posts will be reviewed before they appear on the network. If he breaks the rules too much, his account is deleted. This system weeds out junk posts and junk members.

- Why does LinkedIn allow pods? Because they know members will visit LinkedIn if there is good content. Sociologists have found in all social networks, both on the web and in the real world, about one to two percent of members are the hard core. They create the original ideas of the group. In the arts, they write the music, books, movies, theater, and poetry. In science, they do the original research and discoveries. In computers, the hard core develops the hardware and writes the software. This holds true in all societies worldwide and all activities. For any social group to thrive and grow, it must allow and encourage the hard core to create and spread their ideas. This means LinkedIn allows the key members to increase their visibility.

- Do you need a pod? Absolutely. Pods are the spark to start a fire. If your post doesn't get comments within sixty minutes, your post will disappear. If you get twenty or more comments within sixty minutes, your post will get 500% more views.

- Will you always need to use pods? When you're starting, you need to build an audience. When your followers notice that you write useful content, they will begin on their own to comment and forward your postings. When you're established, you won't need a pod anymore. Until then, use a pod.

Your Post is Trending

When you've done a good job, your post will go viral. LinkedIn will let you know.

Summary

As you saw in this section, you can use posts get attention and build connection with people. LinkedIn has allocated substantial technology and people to ensure that posts are relevant to people, based on their interests. LinkedIn's filters and spam teams also block junk posts. It's good to have a great profile at LinkedIn; it's much better to have a profile and actively post at LinkedIn.

Use LinkedIn Sales Navigator for Outbound Marketing

Up to now, we've looked at LinkedIn from the view of inbound marketing, which means how to get people to come to you in LinkedIn.

Let's now look at the other side of the coin: outbound marketing, which means how to reach out to people in LinkedIn. For B2B lead gen, we want to find, connect, engage, and convert business leads and prospects into business deals.

We do this in LinkedIn with Sales Navigator. In short:

- Sales Navigator has filters to let you search all of your first-, second-, and third-degree connections
- Search by location lets you search by continent, country, state, city, or postal code, along with radius (such as 24 miles/kilometers)
- View each person's profile, background, status, connections, activity, and more so you can decide if the person is a lead or not
- Add the person as a connection
- Add the person to your list of leads
- Be notified whenever your leads take actions, such as update their status, write posts or articles,
- Engage on your leads' actions
- Send InMail messages to your leads

Sales Navigator is a complete platform for lead prospecting and lead gen.

LinkedIn Sales Navigator's advantage over CRM platforms is the ability to see a lead's profile and activity before they have contacted you. Salesforce, SugarCRM, HubSpot, and other CRM tools can collect a visitor's name and information when they visit your website, but they don't include (and can't) complete background information about that visitor. Those CRMs are tools inbound marketing. Sales Navigator is a tool for outbound lead prospecting.

LinkedIn gives you access to professionals around the world. There are 645 million members (July 2019) in more than 200 countries. 160 million members are in the US (half of the US population). By percentage of population, the top countries are US 50%, Netherlands 40%, Canada 38%, UK 35%, Spain 35%, UAE 28%, Sweden 26%, France 23%, Belgium 23%, and Germany 9%. There are 60 million members in India, 40 million in China, and 32 million in Brazil.

LinkedIn Sales Navigator Subscriptions

LinkedIn Sales Navigator (or, as LinkedIn staffers call it, Sales Nav) is an additional paid service in your LinkedIn account.

There are three subscription levels to Sales Navigator:

- Professional: Sales Navigator for your personal LinkedIn account
- Team: If you have (for example) eight people in your sales team, Sales Navigator Team links the eight personal accounts together so you can share your leads and activity with your team
- Enterprise: This integration with CRM such as Salesforce and Microsoft Dynamics 365 for data, monitoring, and reporting activity for each salesperson. The company also owns the accounts, which means if someone leaves, they can't take the

license, conversations, saved leads, and so on to another company.

LinkedIn offers the first month as free trial and afterwards for around $80 per month (depending on monthly payments, one-time annual payment, teams, enterprise, and so on.)

See an overview of the subscriptions at linkedin.com/help/sales-navigator/answer/68183

The rest of this book will look at the use of Sales Navigator for outbound lead gen.

Before we start with Sales Navigator, let's put it in perspective with profiles and posts. Just as you can use Sales Navigator to review a person so you can decide whether to contact them, they too can review your profile, posts, and activity to decide whether to accept your contact request. That's why the first half of this book covered profiles, posts, and activity. You want to be ready before you reach out to others.

Using LinkedIn Sales Navigator

Let's start with the main page in Sales Navigator:

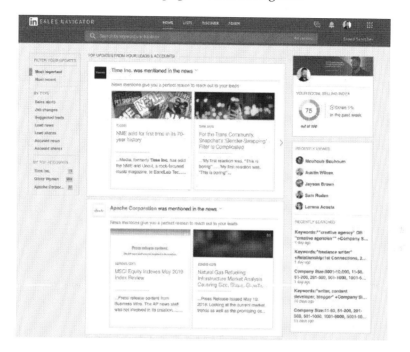

First, let's look at the tabs.

At the right are several buttons that are similar to LinkedIn basic.

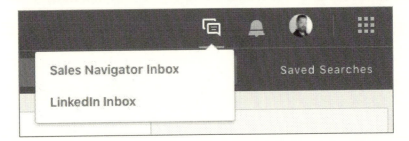

The messages button opens messages for both Sales Navigator Inbox and LinkedIn basics Inbox. You can jump back and forth between the messages.

You can keep your Sales Navigator messages focused on business and use the basic inbox for personal messages.

The bell icon will notify you of new messages, activities, and so on.

These notifications cover your leads and follows on Sales Navigator

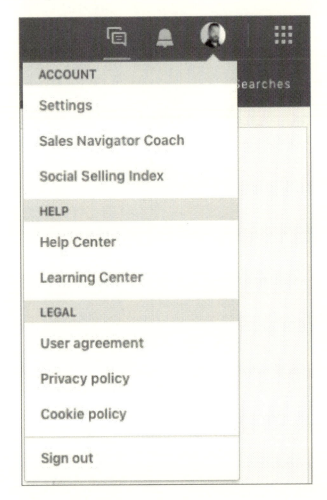

Your Me Icon in Sales Navigator is for Sales Navigator. Here you can:

- Review your account settings
- Get help
- Get information on LinkedIn legal content
- Sign out

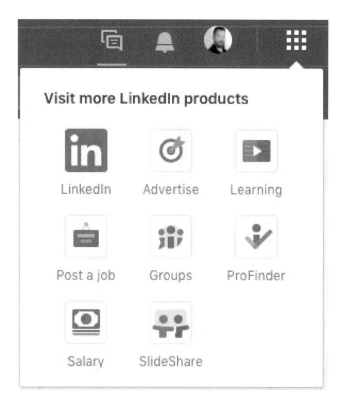

The grid icon has several useful tools. This is also in your basic account. This includes:

- **LinkedIn**: This icon will take you to your home page in LinkedIn basic
- **Advertise**: This icon will take you to LinkedIn's advertising platform. We'll cover this later in this book.
- **Learning**: This icon offers hundreds of thousands of courses on software, tools, business leadership, sales, marketing, and more. Several years ago, LinkedIn bought Lynda.com, a learning platform. When you complete a course, it's often added to your profile.
- **Post a job**: You can post open jobs at your company or consulting practice.

- **Groups:** You can search for groups with keywords and #hashtags, join a group, or start your own group.

- **Profinder:** You can find consultants and freelance contractors for your projects. This includes designers, copywriters, resume writers, SEO, photographers or just about anything. LinkedIn has a vetting process to ensure reliable contractors. If you are a freelance person, you can offer your services. It's also a great way to find a job, as many companies start with contractors who later become staff.

- **Salary**: See the salaries for similar job titles and skills in your area. This is like Glassdoor.com. LinkedIn also shows you available jobs in your market. You will have a stronger position in your next job interview or salary renegotiation.

- **SlideShare:** Yet another place at LinkedIn to share your content. LinkedIn will promote your slides to relevant people.

At the top of Sales Navigator is the search bar.

Start with Sales Navigator by clicking Discover and then click Edit Your Sales Preferences.

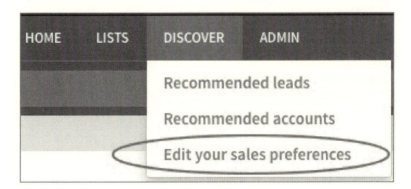

Sales Preferences options include:

- Your account type
- Payment and billing options
- Premium features
- Profile viewing options
- Sales and email preferences

The most important item is sales preferences.

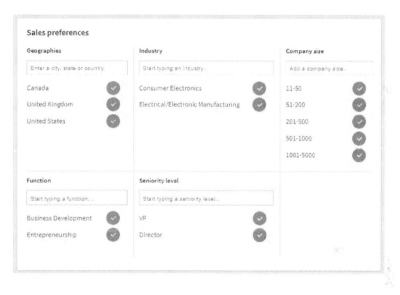

You use Sales Preferences as a set of filters to find people. You set filters for:

- Geographies (city, state, or country)
- Industry
- Company size
- Job Function
- Seniority Level

With the Industry section, choose from 147 fields, including:

- Accounting; airlines/aviation; alternative dispute resolution; alternative medicine; animation; apparel & fashion; architecture & planning; arts and crafts; automotive; aviation & aerospace;

- Banking; biotechnology; broadcast media; building materials; business supplies and equipment;

- Capital markets; chemicals; civic & social organization; civil engineering; commercial real estate; computer & network security; computer games; computer hardware; computer networking; computer software; construction; consumer electronics; consumer goods; consumer services; cosmetics;

- Dairy; defense & space; design;

- E-learning; education management; electrical/electronic manufacturing; entertainment; environmental services; events services; executive office;

- Facilities services; farming; financial services; fine art; fishery; food & beverages; food production; fund-raising; furniture;

- Gambling & casinos; glass, ceramics & concrete; government administration; government relations; graphic design;

- Health, wellness and fitness; higher education; hospital & health care; hospitality; human resources;

- Import and export; individual & family services; industrial automation; information services; information technology and services; insurance; international affairs; international trade and development; internet; investment banking; investment management;

- Judiciary;

- Law enforcement; law practice; legal services; legislative office; leisure, travel & tourism; libraries; logistics and supply chain; luxury goods & jewelry;

- Machinery; management consulting; maritime; market research; marketing and advertising; mechanical or industrial engineering; media production; medical devices; medical practice; mental health care; military; mining & metals; motion pictures and film; museums and institutions; music;
- Nanotechnology; newspapers; nonprofit organization management;
- Oil & energy; online media; outsourcing/offshoring;
- Package/freight delivery; packaging and containers; paper & forest products; performing arts; pharmaceuticals; philanthropy; photography; plastics; political organization; primary/secondary education; printing; professional training & coaching; program development; public policy; public relations and communications; public safety; publishing;
- Railroad manufacture; ranching; real estate; recreational facilities and services; religious institutions; renewables & environment; research; restaurants; retail;
- Security and investigations; semiconductors; shipbuilding; sporting goods; sports; staffing and recruiting; supermarkets;
- Telecommunications; textiles; think tanks; tobacco; translation and localization; transportation/trucking/railroad;
- Utilities;
- Venture capital & private equity; veterinary;
- Warehousing; wholesale; wine and spirits; wireless; and writing and editing.

With the Job Function section, choose from 26 areas, including: accounting; administrative; arts and design; business development; community and social services; consulting; education; engineering; entrepreneurship; finance; healthcare services; human resources; information technology; legal; marketing; media communication; military and protective services; operations; product management; program and project management; purchasing; quality assurance; real estate; research; sales; and support.

You can add multiple items in each section. Check each one to add it to your list. However, the more focused your criteria, the better the results.

The Social Selling Index (SSI)

The Social Selling Index (SSI) shows you at a glance how well you are doing in managing your LinkedIn profile.

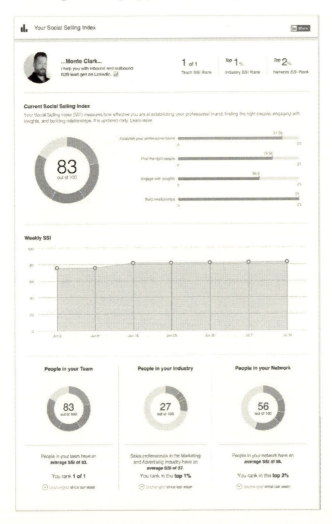

Your SSI has four categories:

- Establishing your professional brand (orange)
- Find the right people (purple)
- Engaging with Insights (red)
- Building relationships (green)

Your SSI score encourages you to improve your profile, which improves your visibility, which improves your reach and connections.

LinkedIn tells you how to improve your score. As you roll over the bar chart items, LinkedIn gives you tips.

When you click the text next to the bar charts, a popup window shows you series of slides on how to improve. For example, click on Establish Your Brand and a set of slides appears. (Note: LinkedIn is part of Microsoft, so the slides appear in Microsoft Edge browsers, but not Google Chrome.)

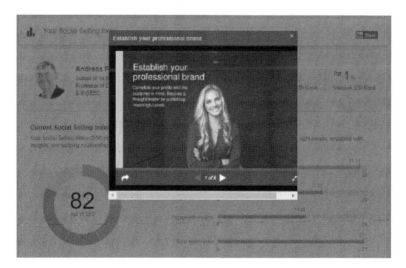

When you have a better score, LinkedIn shows your profile to other highly qualified prospects and shows more leads to you.

LinkedIn also shows you how you compare with other users on LinkedIn, both in your network and in your area of expertise.

If you're part of a business development or sales team at a company, you can tie your Sales Navigator accounts together as a team. This lets your team share leads and contacts. You can also see your SSI score in comparison to your team, which will motivate team members to improve their profiles. This is good for each of you and the team because the better your team's scores, the more opportunities you will find.

Searching Sales Navigator

To start your first search, click Advanced in the Search Bar and choose Search for Leads:

This opens a set of filters to narrow your search:

Because you already set your sales preferences, you can use those preferences for your search. Toggle the "Apply your Sales Preferences" switch at the top right of the box. This populates the necessary fields with your choices.

After making your selections, Sales Navigator will search the network for connections which match your search criteria. Sales Navigator uses your first-, second-, and third-tier connections (which is another reason to accept all requests for connections).

Here is one of the advantages of Sales Navigator: you can find more leads. LinkedIn Basic only shows you 1st degree (your contacts) and 2nd degree (friend of a friend) contacts.

Your contacts have more contacts, which becomes a large number. To find the potential reach of your contact network, go to your LinkedIn Basics account, type an asterisk in the search bar, and press Enter. Andreas has 10,400 contacts, so he can potentially reach 163 million members.

Can you see how many connections someone has? LinkedIn usually only shows you that someone has 500+ connections.

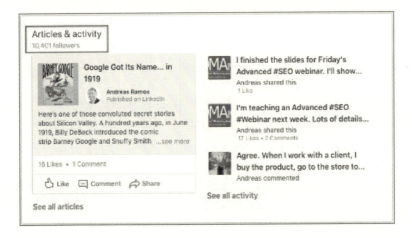

But if you look at a person's recent activity, LinkedIn shows the number of followers. At the top left, you see Andreas has 10,401 followers.

The search will show you a list of results. You can save your work by selecting "Save Search" to the right of the search bar.

If you want more results, change your filter. For example, use different titles, company sizes, and keywords.

After you've completed and saved a few searches, when you click on the search bar at the top of your screen those searches will automatically appear:

- Your previous saved searches will show
- Sales Navigator offers options for additional searches
- Sales Navigator offers additional search tips to find the right leads

Look at your results window. At the top you will find the number of search results and additional information.

The first number may be very large based on your search criteria. As you can see in this example, Monte has 865 total results. This is a very large number to start a campaign with, but if you look to the right you see only 288 of the 865 members posted on LinkedIn the past 30 days. These 288 are active participants, which is also a manageable number of contacts to pursue. You can always add or remove filters to increase or decrease the number of leads.

You can scroll through your results. There are several options that you can use.

You can save a lead by clicking the Save button at the right of the lead. You can create new lead list or select a leads list you've already created.

You can select the three dots, as shown here:

The pulldown menu offers Connect, View Profile, View Similar, or Message.

Start by clicking the person's name. This opens a widow with information about the lead. You can see the person's title and opening paragraph along with a quick summary of current jobs, previous jobs, and education. In addition, you can see who the person reports to and their additional contact information.

You can save the lead or message them directly from this page as well as see any contact information they have provided to LinkedIn. Often, there may be an email address and Twitter ID.

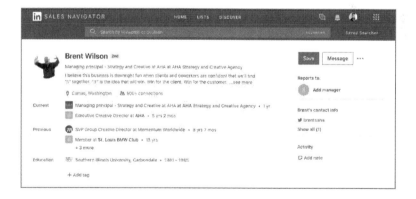

Mastering LinkedIn   85

Clicking the three dots next to the Message box will allow you to connect, add a note, view the profile on LinkedIn, or copy the LinkedIn URL.

At the bottom of the screen, there is the "+Add Tag" button. You can use this to segment your connections into groups. You can add multiple tags for a connection and when you search on your saved leads, you can bring them up by their tags. For instance, you can search "Managing Principal," and bring up all leads that you've tagged with that tag.

Highlights

Highlights show what you have in common with a lead, mutual connections who can make an introduction for you, and the lead's recent activity on LinkedIn. These three boxes of information can give you a strong advantage for you to connect and start a business relationship.

How You Can Use the Highlights Information

You can also use the information about recent activity by clicking on the post and leaving a comment. If you use an @mention with his name, he will get an alert on his mobile phone and see a comment was made. After you make your comment and show you're interested in Brent's postings, you can then use information from the first two boxes to tailor a message to him. This turns a cold lead into a warm lead.

The next block of information shows your lead's work experience. You can see what your lead does and says about their company. Look to the right of your lead's experience to see who else works at the company.

You can connect with those people before connecting to your lead. It's more likely that lower-level people within the company will connect to you. When senior-level people see that you have contacts to people whom they know, they'll accept your connection request. You can also start conversations so you can learn about the company. You could try to learn how the company makes decisions, if budgets have been allocated for products and services, the decision-making timeline, and who is the decision maker. Another way to find contacts at a company is to review from their corporate page on LinkedIn and look for employees.

Tip: Employees who link to their company pages are usually the most pro-active and open people at the company.

Let's look at your lead's skills and endorsements, along with recommendations.

You can use these when you make your connection request. Recommendations are great because if the person is speaking about something the lead did for them, you can let the person know that you'd like to know more about how that went. Anything to get a person to talk about themselves will greatly increase your chances of connecting.

The next section shows your lead's interests.

Look at these to see if there are mutual interests.

We hope you see by now why you should fill out your own profile as much as possible. By listing your job titles, companies, skills, endorsements, groups, and interests, you also give people the opportunity to see if you're the right match for them. You look for people and people also look for you.

In general, people look for the "right cultural fit", which means, will this person fit into our business work culture? Every company has its own culture, based on the field, the people, location and so on. For the same reason that you want to work with people who match your style, they also want to find people who match their style. Therefore you should fill out your profile to give a full picture of what you do.

Yet More Leads

LinkedIn's algorithms use your filters and actions to offer additional leads like the ones that you've chosen.

Look through these to find more leads. Note the "See More" link at the bottom of the box to get more similar leads. Or you can go back and continue reviewing the list of 280 leads that you find in search.

The amount of information is useful for sales, business development, or any kind of outreach. This can also be used for a job search. A single deal easily makes it worthwhile to get a Sales Navigator subscription.

The Sales Navigator Home Page

Once you've started using search and adding people as leads, your home page will start to look like a dashboard, filled with helpful information.

The middle section shows updates from the leads that you've saved. It also shows updates from people who Sales Navigator thinks are your top leads. Sales Navigator will also suggest leads based on your prior searches. You can look at these opportunities and see if there is reason for engagement.

You can modify what you see in the feed by using the filter button on the top right of the feed.

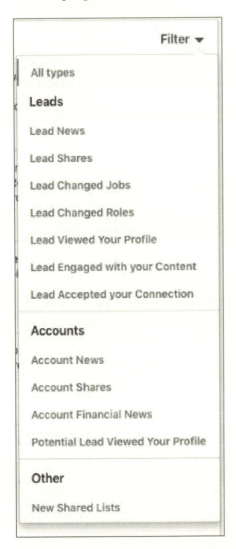

There are many ways to look at the news feed. We prefer to see most recent opportunities over what Sales Navigator feels are our most important, but it's up to you.

When you start with Sales Navigator, most of the items in "By Type" may not have any results. After using Sales Navigator, saving leads, and adding tags, LinkedIn will begin to add results to these.

The last section of this menu shows your top saved accounts and the number of additional opportunities. Clicking these will show all the engagement by the lead for you to review and engage with.

A nice feature of Sales Navigator is that you can use the Sales Navigator feed, which is tailored to your searches and leads, without having to look at the general LinkedIn news feed.

Notice the Saved Searches in the top right next to the search bar. Next to it, a red oval alerts you to more leads that Sales Navigator has found. These are based on your previous searches.

Clicking the Saved Searches link will show a dropdown menu to show you additional leads for your searches.

Lists and Discover

The Lists and Discover navigation menus are next to your home button in your main navigation at the top of your screen.

Both of these menus produce a dropdown menu with additional items.

The Lead Lists option shows your leads by their connection status to you as 1st, 2nd, and 3rd tier connections.

This lets you tag them and sort them into lead groups. For example, you tag the marketing directors with a tag (such as "Marketing Directors), you can enter the tag in search and see all connections with that tag. You can also click the three dots next to the save button to find additional people on LinkedIn who are similar to the connection.

When you view your network in Sales Navigator, you get the same wealth of information about each lead as you saw in the search tool.

Both Lead Lists and Account Lists brings up leads and lists that you have saved.

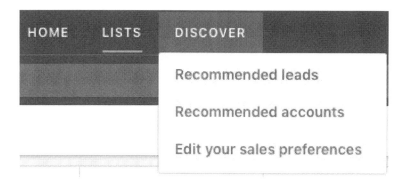

The last item in the list is Edit Your Sales Preferences. This lets you change your sales preferences. This is useful because LinkedIn uses your sales preferences for your results in search and your news feed in Sales Navigator.

Recommended leads are people that Sales Navigator things will be good for you based on your network and sales preferences. Recommended accounts are the companies that Sales Navigator thinks are valuable to you for the same reason.

How We Use Sales Navigator

We don't just talk about Sales Nav. We use it.

- Monte Clark consults with B2B bizdev lead gen teams and individuals to use LinkedIn Sales Navigator. This includes improving profiles for everyone on the sales team, managing Sales Navigator, and creating pods to increase post visibility. Talk with him at MonteClark.com
- Andreas is the CMO at an IoT startup in Palo Alto. Lingolet builds a small device, the size of a cigarette lighter, that translates between twelve languages. It also allows live interpreting for medical, legal, and corporate use. He and the CSO use Sales Navigator find and manage leads. See Lingolet.com

Summary of LinkedIn Sales Navigator

As you can see from everything that we've written up to now in this book, the more you put into LinkedIn and Sales Navigator, the more you get from it.

As you improve your profile, your activity (comments, posts, articles), and your Sales Navigation preferences and leads lists, the better LinkedIn's algorithms understand you and match you with others. You will get highly-targets lead opportunities; you will be visible to the top accounts.

People look for reliable, trustworthy business partners with expertise in a field. This is what you also want. Your profile should show that. Focus on building your real-world skills and credentials and make sure your LinkedIn profile shows that.

Use Sales Navigator to find other experts with whom you can do business. You can see from their profiles that they're the one you want; they can see in your profile that they can work with you.

Use LinkedIn Ads for Outbound Marketing

Another form of outbound marketing is advertising. You use ads to reach people.

Use the Work button to open LinkedIn advertising.

Let's start by looking at how LinkedIn manages campaigns. We'll also look at how to create a strategy.

There are several types of campaigns:

- **Sponsored Content Post:** Sponsored Content Posts are ads that use your own post. You pay to distribute your posts. These are shown in the news feed.

- **Sponsored InMail:** You can use Sponsored InMail to send an email newsletter to your contacts. These appear in your target audience's messages.

- **Video Ads:** The most effective ad format is video. If you create good quality video, then video ads are for you.

- **Text Ads:** Text ads include a small logo. These show up in LinkedIn at the top and side of the page.

- **Dynamic Ads:** Dynamic ads let you use a profile's profile data, such as photo, company name, job title, and more in your ad. These appear in a user's profile page.

- **Carousel Ads:** Carousel ads show a series of images that a user can scroll. These allow you to show several products or a series of messages.

- **Display Ads:** Display ads are also known as banner ads or image ads.

Which is the best? It depends on your market and audience. Try different formats to see what works best.

Use LinkedIn Advertising to Boost your Posts and Articles

LinkedIn ads give you another way to boost engagement of your posts and articles.
1. Write your post or article in LinkedIn
2. Get the URL for your post or article
3. Create an ad to promote the posting or article

An ad in the first 24-48 hours can increase your post distribution to tens of thousands. You can use this along with your comment pod.

How the Bidding System Works

In 2002, Google introduced the Vickrey auction bidding system to develop Google Ads. It was so successful that all online advertising uses a version of Vickrey bidding. Instead of ranking ads by simply looking at who bids the most, Vickrey bidding looks at ad metrics. Google looks at the keyword's click-through-rate (CTR), the ad's CTR, and the bounce rate. Bounce rate means you clicked on an ad, went to a landing page, didn't click further, and returned to Google. That indicates the landing page was not sufficiently interesting. Google also uses conversion tracking to look at conversion rates.

Why does Google do this? Let's say there are two competitors. One bids $5 and the other bids $2. In traditional ad bidding, the $5 ad will be at the top. However, it has weak keywords and a poor ad. In contrast, the $2 uses top keywords and a well-written ad that appeals to the visitor. She clicks the ad, arrives at a landing page which offers what she wants, and she buys. The advertiser sees that Google Ads help sales, so he'll increase his budget. Google also sees the $2 may be lower in price, but it gets more clicks, so Google ranks the $2 ad above the $5 ad.

LinkedIn uses somewhat the same for its advertising. The factors include:

- Likes
- Views
- Time on post
- Comments
- Sentiment of comments
- Shares

LinkedIn also looks at how many connections you have, the quality of your connections with regards to your market, how many followers you have, and your overall activity. They look at CTR, bounce back, and conversion rates. They look at member feedback, such as people who hide your posts from their feed or report your post.

Let's look at an example of bidding.

- Let's say Monte bids $8.00
- Andreas bids $12.00
- It appears Andreas wins

But Monte's relevance score is 9 and Andreas's score is 4. LinkedIn multiplies the bid price and the relevance score to get a combined score:

- Monte: $8 x Relevance Score 9 = 72 Points
- Andreas: $12 x Relevance Score 4 = 48 Points

Monte wins the auction because he has a higher score.

What about the cost-per-click? LinkedIn takes the next highest point (in this case, Andreas' 48 points) and divides by Monte's relevance score (9):

- Andreas's Score 48 / Monte's Relevance Score 9 = $5.34 Monte's Cost per Click
- Monte's ad will show up higher and more often, even though he bids less than Andreas' bid

So, although Andreas is willing to pay more, Monte will get more clicks, so LinkedIn will earn more money on the lower bid.

This is also good for the users. In this case, Monte writes better ads than Andreas, which is better for users.

Does Monte win every time? No, it all depends on the market. In other areas, Andreas may have better score so his ads will be cheaper than Monte's and show up higher.

Tip: The same bidding process exists in Google, Facebook, Bing, and so on. Silicon Valley companies either learn from each other or people move from company to company and bring ideas. Soon after Google started this bidding process, it spread to all sites that offer advertising. If you use digital advertising, you must learn how it works. The best campaign, not the top bid, wins the game, which means a well-managed campaign with a small budget and low bids can beat its competitors.

Note: Andreas teaches how the Vickrey auction system works at Google Ads. When you understand this, you can write ads that rank higher than your competitors, you can bid less than your competitors, and have lower budgets, yet get more clicks. These university-level online webinars cover SEO, Google Ads, Google Analytics, and other topics. You get the presentation files, audio recording, and ebooks.

For more, see andreas.com/digital-marketing-webinars.html

Bid Options

You can pay for ads in two ways:

- CPM (Cost per Thousand): You pay to show 1,000 ads
- CPC (Cost-per-Click): You pay only if someone clicks the ad

It's up to you. Try both and see what works best.

But Don't People Say LinkedIn Ads Are Expensive?

Many say LinkedIn ads aren't effective and too expensive.

As you can see, if someone doesn't understand the system, the ads will indeed be expensive and won't show much.

If you have a great profile, a good network, lots of activity, and good decoration, your ads will work much better.

Let's look at how you make an ad on LinkedIn.

After you've created an account and click Create Campaign, LinkedIn will guide you through a step-by-step process of creating your first ad.

Step #1: Name your campaign. Name your campaign group and your campaign name. Many accounts have multiple groups and multiple campaigns within each group.

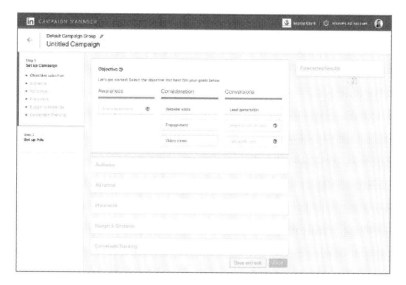

Step #2: Select your objective. You can choose Consideration or Conversions (LinkedIn will soon add "Awareness").

Under Consideration your options are:

- Website visits: Visits to your website
- Engagement: More followers of your LinkedIn Content
- Video views: More views of your video posts. A video post counts a view when someone has watched more than ten seconds.

You can use both strategies with LinkedIn Ads. In fact, I recommend that both of these strategies be engaged simultaneously. If your budget allows, you should have some ads that are lead generation, and some that build awareness and your connections.

The next step is your audience. LinkedIn has a feature that will help you with this step and created audience groups that you can select from. Some of these are broad, such as, "Members with a bachelor's degree." Others are narrow, such as, "Expertise in Biotechnology." You can scroll through their list and see if LinkedIn has already created a group for you, or you can search a group by keyword.

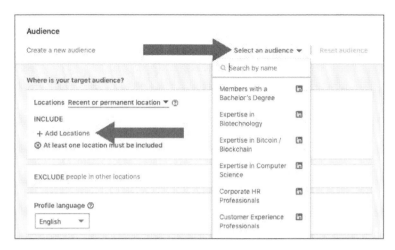

If you select a predefined audience from the LinkedIn list, it will auto populate your audience field. Add an audience defined by LinkedIn to see what they include, and then remove or add additional items.

Next, narrow that group by location. You can choose or exclude states/provinces or cities within countries.

Set the language. English is the global language for business, technology, science, and other fields. For some countries, you may add additional languages.

If you didn't choose a preselected audience from the pulldown, you can add your audience with keywords.

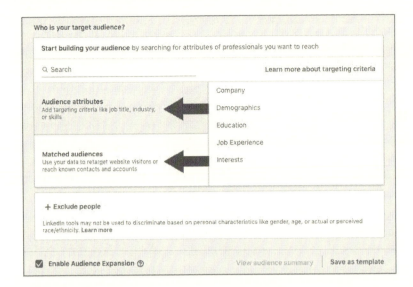

LinkedIn will help you to create your audience with Audience attributes and Matched audiences.

Audience attributes breaks down your audience by company, demographics, education, job experience, and interests.

Matched audience uses your website's traffic. To use Matched Audience, add LinkedIn tracking code to your site. In addition, LinkedIn allows you to upload your own lists from contacts or other accounts, and even integrates with CRM platforms such as HubSpot.

Once you've made these selections, you can exclude profiles such as existing customers or competitors who you don't want to see your ad.

Clicking Enable Audience Expansion allows LinkedIn to add to your audience based on the parameters you've defined.

If you are creating multiple versions of the campaign for testing, you can save the template and load it to make quick adjustments. You can make many different versions of the campaign and test each to see which audience performs the best.

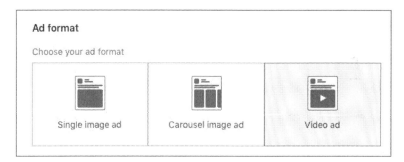

Next, select an ad format. There are three options:

Clicking Enable the LinkedIn Audience Network allows LinkedIn to show your ad across its partner network. If you uncheck this your ad will only show on LinkedIn. If there are areas that you don't want your ad shown that you then include those sites and apps using the "+ Exclude categories" and "+upload a block list" sections.

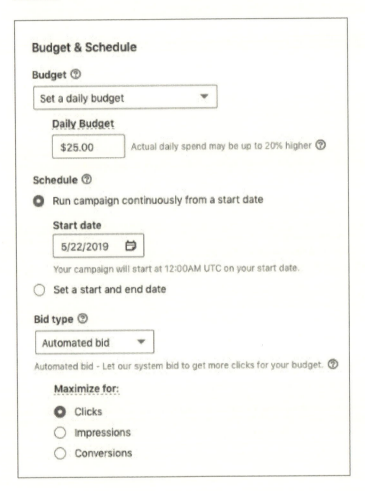

In the Budget and Schedule section first set either a daily budget or set both daily and total budget. If you select both daily and total budget from the dropdown menu, you won't need an end date to your campaign. The campaign will end when your budget has been reached.

If you select set a daily budget, you should select a start and end date. This lets you set up a campaign in advance, for example for a trade show. If you don't set an end date, the campaign will run indefinitely.

How it works
- Our system uses historical campaign data and member information to automatically set your campaign's bid. We recommend using this option to get more clicks for your budget. Learn more

When to use
- When you're not sure how much to bid.
- Get more clicks for your budget than Maximum CPC Bid.
- Aim to fully deliver your budget.

Things to remember
- Your effective CPC could increase as you increase your budget.
- This is charged by impression.
- You cannot set a bid cap.

In the Bid type dropdown, select:

- Automated Bid
- Maximum CPC (cost-per-click) Bid
- Maximum CPM (Cost per 1,000 impressions)

LinkedIn provides helpful information about their automated bid process. We suggest a campaign using LinkedIn to determine the bid and then copying the campaign and doing it yourself. Within a week, you should know which is the best option.

The last step in setting up your campaign is conversion tracking.

> **Conversion tracking (optional)** ⓘ
> Measure the actions members take on your website after clicking or viewing your LinkedIn ad.
> ✛ Add conversions

Conversion tracking follows the actions taken on your ad onto your website. If you want users to download a PDF document, fill out a form, or complete a purchase, you can apply LinkedIn's code to those pages and add the pages to the conversion tracking section.

After you've completed your campaign setup, save it and make several copies of the campaign. Now select the copies and modify the parameters of the campaign or modify the ads in the campaign.

Before creating your first ad, LinkedIn will predict your campaign performance based on past data performance of similar campaigns.

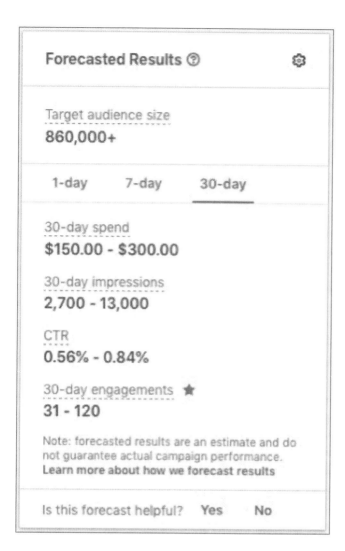

Copy your campaigns, change parameters of them, and look at forecast results. Forecast results is one way to improve your campaign.

Take a screenshot of your forecasted results and compare them to your actual results. Follow these predictions over time, along with your actual analytics to determine if your relevance score is improving or decreasing.

Creating an Ad

After setting up the campaign parameters, create the ad itself. You can either create a new ad or you can browse existing content for your ad. When choosing to browse existing content, the only option available are articles you've posted to your LinkedIn account.

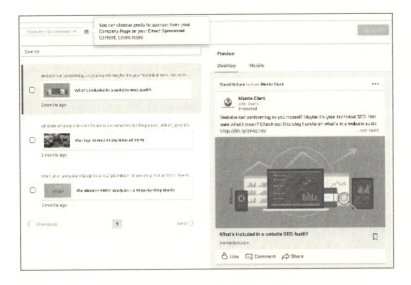

A list of articles created will appear on the left-hand side with a preview of how your ad will appear on the right. If you have a company page, you can also select posts from the company page.

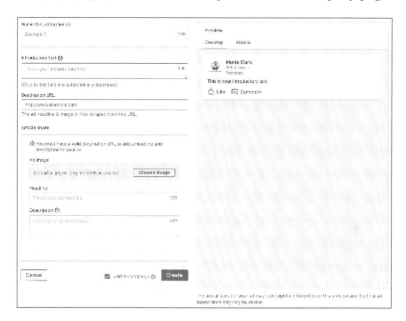

When creating a new ad, notice that the preview shows the ad is from your company page. Ads are only available from company pages or from Showcase pages. When creating a new ad, you can use content from an external website or a LinkedIn article. The ad editor will scrape a photo from the page or you can add a photo.

When creating your ad:

- Research your keywords to find the most-frequently used words
- Put your keyword at the beginning of the title
- Use your keyword in the ad's text
- If you are linking to an external URL, remember to add the LinkedIn tracking code to that page's HTML
- Use an image that draws attention

Lead Gen Forms

To add a form to your ad, create it in your campaign manager.

Find the Lead Gen Forms in Campaign Manager under the Account Assets dropdown menu.

Once you've created your form, when someone clicks your ad, the form will appear. You can create multiple forms and assign them to a specific ad. LinkedIn will auto-populate the form with the user's profile information. All the person has to do is accept and they're done.

Campaign Analytics

You've seen how LinkedIn provides you with post and profile view analytics. In addition, LinkedIn provides campaign analytics on the platform itself and if you install the site analytics will also track behavior from ads to websites.

After your ad has been running a for a day, you can begin to watch the analytics to determine its performance. Click Campaign Performance, and then double click your campaign.

Across the top of the spreadsheet click the various pulldown menus to modify the sections you can view. On the Columns pulldown, we typically keep "performance" selected as it gives us an overall understanding of how the ad is doing.

Under Breakdown, choosing "on off network," displays LinkedIn's audience network, LinkedIn itself, and if you've applied the site tracking code, your website performance.

Last, select a time range for the analytics data. Easily switch between campaigns by selecting them at the top. You can open multiple campaigns for comparison or performance, create a new campaign from this page, and if you roll over the campaign name, a pop-out menu will appear with manage, chart, and duplicate options. Click Chart to see your data. Click Manage to open the ad parameters that you can change.

LinkedIn doesn't show ads in the first spot on the news feed. The second spot is often an ad. There are ads every five to seven posts.

If you are going to engage in advertising on LinkedIn, it would be beneficial to scroll through the feed for a week or so and note the types of ads different companies are running. Also, note the number of followers and likes. Companies with high followers and likes get a better score. Watch what they do so that you can compete.

It's also a good idea to research your competitors' keywords and hashtags. You can do this on Google and see where your competitors rank in search. It's most likely they will use the same keywords across social platforms as well.

Make a spreadsheet with your competitors' headlines, descriptions, and what they use for graphics. In addition, note their offer, what They're trying to achieve with their ads, what they ask users do such as fill in a LinkedIn form, go to a website, or get more followers.

Finally, connect to and follow their followers. If people follow your competitor, they will likely follow you as well. If there are comments to the ad, check the comments and engage with them. Again, if someone engaged your competitors' ad, they will likely engage with you.

Summary

People who try to power their way into LinkedIn with lots of ads and a big budget will find cost-per-click (CPC) are high because the account's quality score is very low. By understanding the LinkedIn advertising, you can get low CPC and good results.

We suggest that you use LinkedIn advertising to support your presence on the platform. Maintain a great profile, write relevant, interesting posts, and use pods to boost your posts. Use advertising to drive traffic to your posts to get thousands of views.

Extras for LinkedIn: Crystal

Use Crystal for Personality Analysis

Crystal offers a personality analysis based on a person's LinkedIn profile. Crystal is a third-party plugin for the Chrome browser. The free version can analyze ten LinkedIn accounts. Get unlimited personality assessments with the paid version at $40 per month.

Crystal is by another company and not part of LinkedIn. Get Crystal at CrystalKnows.com

A Crystal personality profile tells you:

- How a person communicates
- How you should lead a conversation
- The kind of responses you may expect when communicating
- How long it may take to establish a relationship
- How to adjust your personality to their personality
- How your lead will likely to respond to your invitation
- How long it may take for a lead, to convert to a sale

After you install the Chrome browser plugin and open LinkedIn, a blue tab appears at the right. When you open someone's profile page, Crystal automatically analyses the profile.

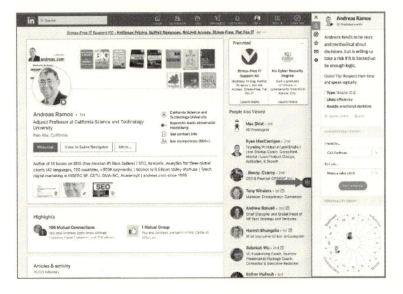

Let's look at an example. (Wait, Monte is using me as a test rabbit?)

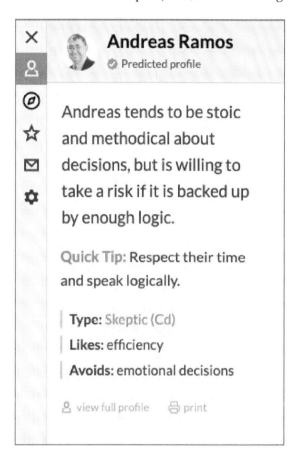

The summary is a quick overview of who you are dealing with. The Quick Tip tells you how to talk with Andreas.

The Conversation Coach will suggest how to talk with someone. Your "need to" options are to call, send an email, or have a meeting.

The "So, I can" responses include:

- Make a sales pitch
- Negotiate
- Make a good impression
- Schedule a meeting
- Discuss pricing
- Deliver bad news
- Resolve a conflict
- Give feedback
- Collaborate on a project
- Brainstorm ideas

- Give instructions
- Ask for a raise
- Convince them to hire you

The Crystal personality graph shows the four main personality traits for your contact.

When you sign up with Crystal, you answer a series of questions to find your own personality profile. When you use Crystal assessments on LinkedIn contacts, Crystal will match your profile against theirs.

The closer to the center for you, the better you will be to accommodate the other person. The further out you are, the more difficult it will be to work with the other person.

You can see Andreas is in the middle of Conscientious dominant. The small "d" means he has a small amount of dominant tendencies but he's mostly Conscientious. Monte is between Dominant and Dominant influential and at the small inner circle of the graph. This means while Monte is mostly dominant, he will have an easy time working with other personalities.

Crystal gives you suggestions on how to approach communication with others.

The Relationship graph gives you additional ideas. It uses the same data as the disc graph but in a different presentation.

Monte can use this to see how to have a conversation with Andreas:

- Monte is more risk-tolerant than Andreas. While Andreas isn't completely risk-averse, it will take more to convince him if there are any risks.

- You would think that since Monte is risk-tolerant, he would be more trusting. But, that's not the case. In the second parameter, you see Andreas and Monte are both skeptics, so both of them will want to see proof before they make decisions.

- You can see Andreas is deliberate while Monte is fast paced. This gives insight into how long it might take to make a sale with Andreas. Typically, someone who is fast paced, such as Monte, will assume there is a problem if he doesn't close a sale on the first phone call. However, Andreas is deliberate, so it may take several weeks before Monte hears from Andreas.

- This graph shows Andreas is Matter of Fact, while Monte is Expressive. To be successful with Andreas, Monte needs to stick to concrete evidence. Andreas won't like drawn out creative ways around an issue.

As you can see, Crystal gives Monte an idea of how to communicate with Andreas, what motivates Andreas, and what it would be like to work with him.

ANDREAS' PERSONALITY

Overview

Andreas is likely to focus on execution and efficiency, favoring independence over collaboration and consensus. This can be a wonderful asset when pressed for time, but can potentially create conflict with others who need to be involved in decisions.

It comes naturally for **Andreas**

Question inefficient practices

Highly value accuracy

Verbally challenge a bold claim about a product

Communication

Make sure to use data when trying to prove your point. Expect Andreas to challenge you, and be prepared to present proven facts and statistics instead of stories and anecdotes.

When speaking to **Andreas**

Set clear expectations for the conversation

Trust that . they will follow specific verbal instructions

Stay objective rather than emotional

In summary, Crystal is a good add-on for Sales Navigator. Use Sale Navigator to find people and use Crystal to get ideas on how to work with them.

Summary: So... What's Next?

While writing this book, we had many late-night discussions between ourselves and with our friends about what's going on with websites, search engines, social media, and other things. Here are a few notes from these discussions.

To understand where the web is going, let's look at how it started and where it is today.

Websites started in the early 90s. By 2005, there were thousands of sites. Those first websites were brochureware: the website was pretty much just a paper brochure on the web with a logo, a heading, a few pictures, some text, and contact information.

By the late 90s, graphics designers got on the web and there was an explosion of exuberant creativity in web design. Many of these sites were almost a type of abstract art.

Twenty years later... no more creativity. Nearly all websites today have the same structure and functions. We're pretty much back to brochureware.

Why? Amazon. If you're selling stuff, there's not much point in building and managing a website with database, transaction tools, and so on because consumers go to Amazon to buy stuff. Amazon Prime and one-click shopping lets people buy without having to register, fill out address forms, enter credit cards, verify, and so on. One click, done. Goodbye, creative websites.

When the web grew to thousands of pages in 1994-5, there arose the need for some way to find webpages. Soon there were more than 200 search engines. Google added advertising in 2001 and quickly made so much money that other search engines faded away. Today, there are only a handful of search engines: Google, Bing, Baidu, Yandex, and DuckDuckGo. But the same thing happened to search engines: after the burst of creativity, search had pretty much been solved by 2006-9. There haven't been any further significant advances in search.

Social media has experienced the same evolution. Social started around 2002 and within a few years, there were hundreds, if not thousands, of social sites. In 2019, seventeen years later, most are gone. Andreas manages web analytics for a global site; he can see in analytics that traffic comes from only 61 social sites and we doubt you can name more than ten of them. Underneath the surface, social media sites are pretty much the same.

Folks, we didn't expect this. When the web started in the early 90s, we thought everyone would have a personal website. Some of you may remember the slogan, "a level playing field on the Internet Superhighway". Instead, the web consolidated into a few global giant companies and the evolution stopped.

That's where we're at today.

Andreas' university students always ask, "what's next?"

There are several answers.

First, Silicon Valley is shifting again. From 1940 to 1990, Silicon Valley was silicon: it made hardware, such as integrated circuits, computer chips, disk drives, and so on. In the mid-90s, Silicon Valley became Internet Valley, which shifted to web companies, such as Yahoo!, Google, Facebook, Amazon, and others. But that market is full. User growth has flattened since 2016.

A second answer: Silicon Valley used to be Santa Clara Valley, an actual valley between two low mountain ranges. Many cities and countries around the world spent billions of dollars to build their own Silicon Valleys but none of those happened. By 2005, Silicon Valley grew to include San Francisco and the greater San Francisco Bay Area and, somewhere around 2015, Silicon Valley spread to the rest of the world. You can be anywhere now with digital technology and the web. Skype, GoToMeeting, Zoom, Google Hangout, WeChat, and many more let you talk with your team, investors, and customers anywhere on the planet. You can easily transfer money. People build startups in France, China, and Colombia and fly to Silicon Valley for meetings with investors and lawyers. The focus shifted to building global products, teams, and markets.

Which brings up several more answers. The first is IoT. These devices are embedded to larger products to collect data, share data, and make decisions. Any car built in the last few years has hundreds, if not thousands, of embedded IoT chips that monitor and adjust the car's performance. There's a clue in what's coming by looking at the number of IP addresses. An IP address is the phone number, so to speak, of a connected device. The old IPv4 standard allowed 4.3 billion devices. Yes, not much. The new IPv6 standard allows 3.4×10^{38} devices. That's 340 trillion trillion trillion or the number of cat hairs on your new suit. IoT will be bigger than the last twenty years of the web.

Another answer is blockchain. Distributed ledger technology (DLT) will allow the tracking of practically everything and ensure verification. Bitcoin is just one minor (but very loud) aspect of blockchain; hundreds of companies around the world are building blockchain solutions as fast as possible.

So where is LinkedIn in all of this? It seems to us that personal websites are turning into a type of business card: you have one so people can contact you. But just as you needed search engines to find websites in 1995, you need a way to find people today. And not just anyone: you want to find the few hundred relevant professional connections. There must also be a way to ensure they are real people with actual credentials.

For so long, we thought LinkedIn was just a resume database for recruiters.

But LinkedIn has been adding tools and features, plus it built a robust filter that uses both AI machine learning and people to block spammers and fraud.

Sales Navigator is much more than some sort of "Google for resumes"; you can use it to find people and see their background, activity, postings, connections, skills, and more. It lets you monitor the person's activity until you're ready to connect and it gives you the tools to connect. There's nothing else like this.

We're glad we wrote this book because it let us learn about Sales Nav in detail so we can use it for our work and clients. We hope it will do the same for you.

In Closing

We want to thank you for reading our book. We learned a lot in writing this and we hope you'll be able to apply some of this to your business so you can get some more sales, make a bit more money, and have a happier life for yourself and your family.

Monte in Kansas City
Andreas in Palo Alto
August 5th, 2019

Email Us

Questions, comments, ideas? Speaker for your next conference or event? Talk with us.

- Monte@MonteClark.com
- andeas@andreas.com

Get Help with LinkedIn

- Monte Clark consults with B2B bizdev lead gen teams to use and manage LinkedIn Sales Navigator. This includes improving profiles for everyone on a sales team, managing Sales Navigator, and creating pods to increase visibility. Talk with him at MonteClark.com
- Andreas teaches university-level online webinars on SEO, Google Ads, Google Analytics, and other topics. You get the presentation files, audio recording, and ebooks. For more, see Andreas.com/digital-marketing-webinars.html

Connect with Us at LinkedIn

- Monte Clark at LinkedIn.com/in/MonteClark
- Andreas Ramos at LinkedIn.com/in/AndreasRamos

More Information about LinkedIn

There are many useful webpages at LinkedIn. Here are several:

- linkedin.com/company/grant-thornton-llp/
- engineering.linkedin.com
- linkedin.com/help/linkedin
- business.linkedin.com/sales-solutions
- business.linkedin.com/sales-solutions/blog

LinkedIn Customer Support

- For help with LinkedIn, go to your Me menu, click customer support, and send an email.
- For a quick response, use Twitter at twitter.com/LinkedInHelp (@LinkedInHelp) and you'll get a quick response.

Add the LinkedIn Alert to Your Browser

- You can add a LinkedIn alert to your Chrome browser, so you know when there are new notifications. Install it at https://t2m.io/nQtSVdd3m

Notes, Ideas, Dreams

Made in the USA
Middletown, DE
23 August 2019